Connecticut

CONNECTICUT BY ROAD

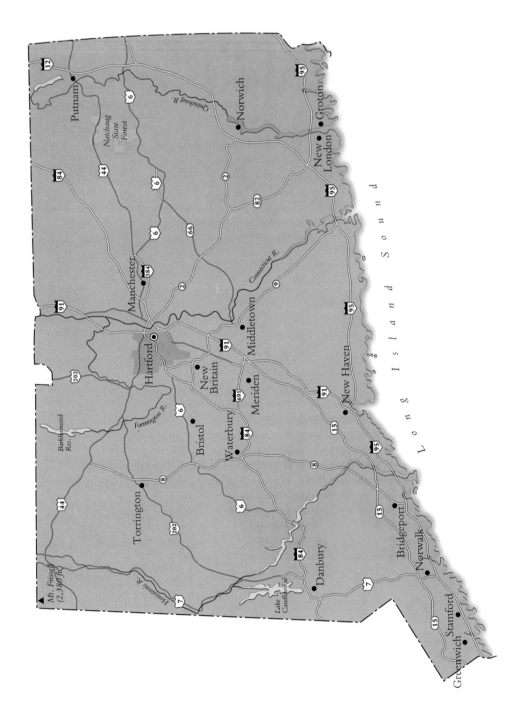

Celebrate the States

Connecticut

Victoria Sherrow

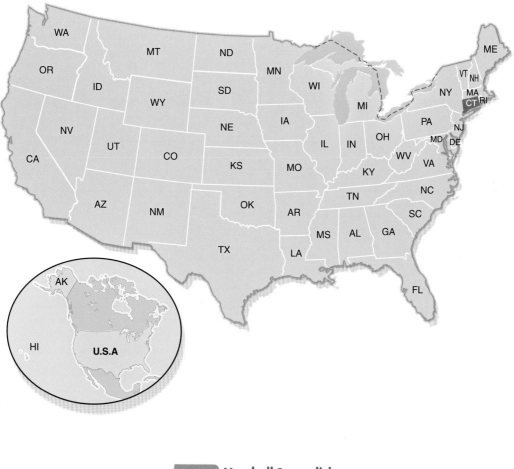

mc **Marshall Cavendish**
Benchmark
New York

Marshall Cavendish Corporation
99 White Plains Road
Tarrytown, New York 10591-9001
www.marshallcavendish.us

All Internet sites were correct and accurate at the time of printing.

Library of Congress Cataloging-in-Publication Data
Sherrow, Victoria.
Connecticut / by Victoria Sherrow.—2nd ed.
p. cm.—(Celebrate the states)
Summary: "Provides comprehensive information on the geography, history, wildlife, governmental structure, economy, cultural diversity, peoples, religion, and landmarks of Connecticut"—Provided by publisher.
Includes bibliographical references and index.
ISBN-13: 978-0-7614-2155-9
ISBN-10: 0-7614-2155-6
1. Connecticut—Juvenile literature. I. Title. II. Series.
F94.3.S54   2006   974.6—dc22   2005029048

Editor: Christine Florie
Editorial Director: Michelle Bisson
Art Director: Anahid Hamparian
Series Designer: Adam Mietlowski
Photo research by Candlepants Incorporated

Cover Photo: Richard Cummins/Superstock

The photographs in this book are used by permission and through the courtesy of; *Corbis:* David Muench, 8; Phil Schermeister, 11, 14, 20; Gabe Palmer, 12; Viviane Moos, 15; Raymond Gehman, 17, 96; Ted Horowitz, 18; Gary W. Cater, 19; Cloud Hills Imaging Ltd.,21; Joseph Sohm, 23; Todd Gipstein, 25, 91, 134; 48, 74, 88, 126, 127, 129, 133; James Marshall, 60, 123; Steve Sands, 68; Greg Flume, 71; Catherine Karnoow, 95; Brian Snyder, 98; Lee Snider, 105; Dale C. Spartas, 111; Arthur Morris, 115(top); Hal Horwitz, 115(low); W. Perry Conway, 119; William Coupon, 128; David Bergman, 130; Bill Collins, 131; Michael T. Sedam, back cover. *Gregory G. Dimijian, M.D./Photo Researchers Inc.:* 26. *The Bridgeman Art Library:* National Gallery of Art, Washington DC, USA , 28; Florence Griswold Museum, Old Lyme, Connecticut, USA/ Gift of the Hartford Steam Boiler Inspection & Insurance Co., 86. *North Wind Picture Archive:* 31, 33, 34, 36. 38, 40, 42, 47. *The Image Works:* Andre Jenny, 37, 103, 109; Peter Hvizdak, 54, 63, 64, 75, 76, 80, 106, 113; Michael J. Doolittle, 56, 57, 58, 67, 82, 84 Arnold Gold, 69; Joseph Sohm, 72; Mary Evans Picture Library, 89. *Getty Images:* Peter Stackpole, 52. *AP/Wide World Photos;* 92. *Superstock:* Stuart Small, 100.

Printed in China
3 5 6 4 2

Contents

Connecticut Is . . .   6

Chapter One   9
Geography: Natural Wonders
Plentiful Waters ▪ Rocks ▪ Woods ▪ Climate ▪ Plants and Animals ▪ Caring for the Water and Land

Chapter Two   29
History: A History of Resourcefulness
Early Settlers ▪ A Document for Freedom ▪ A Growing Colony ▪ Fighting for Freedom ▪ African Americans ▪ Growth of a State ▪ Part of the Union Army ▪ Into the Twentieth Century ▪ New Challenges

Chapter Three   55
People: Living in the Nutmeg State
A Diverse Population ▪ Two Connecticuts ▪ Coping with Crime ▪ Religious Beliefs ▪ Native Americans ▪ Rich Traditions ▪ Year-Round Activities

Chapter Four   73
Government: Government in the State of Steady Habits
Inside Government ▪ Local Government ▪ National Politics ▪ Meeting Social Needs

Chapter Five   85
Economy: A Changing Economy
From Farms to Factories ▪ Military and Transportation ▪ Financial Industries ▪ Agriculture ▪ Fishing and Aquaculture ▪ Economic Challenges

Chapter Six   101
Landmarks: Places to Visit
Fairfield County and the Gold Coast ▪ New Haven County ▪ Middlesex County ▪ The Submarine Capital ▪ Hartford and Central Connecticut ▪ Hills and Village Greens

State Survey   115

Find Out More   139

Index   141

Connecticut Is . . .

Connecticut is a land of small towns and large cities, of farms and factories . . .

"Blocks and blocks of red brick buildings house the mills and factories that turn the wheels of Bridgeport."

—author Philip Hamburger

"If our land is rich, we are rich, for abundance is at our control."

—agricultural expert Honorable Thomas Butler, 1856

. . . and a diverse state where newcomers from many lands live with people who can trace their ancestry back thousands of years.

"[Our Manchester neighborhood] really was Irish—one-third or maybe one-half, was Irish. [And] lots of Italians at that time, too. . . . The Polish, Lithuanians, and Italians lived mainly in the north end of town."

—Irish-American textile worker Lucy Addy Richardson

"Life was hard and many of our people struggled to survive, yet they clung to their identity and their culture and refused to surrender our reservation land or accept termination."

—Eastern Pequot Indians of Connecticut leader Marcia Jones Flowers

People here tend to prize their independence.

"Connecticut, like most of New England, has a lot of free-thinkers, often cantankerous and opinionated people. And most Connecticut people prize that quality in others."

—journalist Harrison E. Salisbury

Connecticut values its history and traditions while looking toward the future . . .

"We need to continue to rebuild our cities and help them be the economic, cultural, and social forces they have the potential to be."

—Congressman Christopher Shays

"In driving and hiking some 30,000 miles within its boundaries in the past year and a half, I have come to appreciate the beauties of our state, as well as to respect the balance between growth and preservation."

—author William Hubbell

Connecticut is a state of contrasts, where colonial charm meets modern industry. Old church spires, quaint village squares, historic monuments, and homes stand within blocks of superhighways, manufacturing plants, modern sports complexes, and steel-and-glass high-rises. Densely populated cities border deep forests and large areas of open land.

Life in Connecticut has changed greatly since the first white settlers arrived in the 1600s. People from around the globe now live and work in the place that inspired high praise from nineteenth-century French traveler and author Alexis de Tocqueville: "This [little state] you call Connecticut is one very great miracle to me."

Chapter One

Natural Wonders

Sitting at the southernmost part of New England, Connecticut once was a land of steep mountains. That changed tens of thousands of years ago as melting glaciers and heavy rains began to erode the mountains, forming hills and valleys. Except for a narrow coastal plain, there is little flat or empty land in Connecticut's 5,544 square miles. Its most prominent hills include the New England Uplands, which rise in the east and west, and the Taconic Mountains in the northwest. The land is dotted with forests, rocks, ravines, and waterways.

Long Island Sound, an arm of the Atlantic Ocean, borders Connecticut to the south. The land rises gradually from this shoreline, with its long sandy beaches and small wooded islands. Massachusetts forms the northern border. Rhode Island lies on the east and New York borders Connecticut on the west.

PLENTIFUL WATERS

Access to water has strongly influenced where people choose to settle in Connecticut. Water has aided the transportation of both people and goods while also providing energy for industry and fish for food.

Connecticut's landscape is hilly with elevations as high as two thousand feet.

The first European settlers realized that ships could dock easily along the ocean coastline, which provided an easy link between Connecticut and other ports. In 1680 English colonists praised New London as the finest sheltered harbor on the coast. They wrote to English officials, "Ships of great [size] may com up to the town and lye secure in any winds [*sic*]." Of the New London (or Pequot) River, they said, "A ship of 500 tunn may go up to the Towne, and com so near the shore that they may toss a biskit ashoare: and vessells of about 30 tunn may pass up about 12 miles above N. London . . . [*sic*]."

In all, Connecticut has 8,400 miles of rivers and streams, including three major systems. The Housatonic River waters western Connecticut, while the Thames River flows in the eastern part of the state. The Connecticut River is the longest river in New England. It rises near the Canadian border and forms a boundary between New Hampshire and Vermont, then flows across western Massachusetts and central Connecticut before reaching Long Island Sound at Old Saybrook. Along this river valley lies some of the most fertile farmland in the United States east of the Mississippi River.

More than one thousand lakes are strewn across the state's surface. Most of them were formed thousands of years ago, when the glaciers that had covered the land during the Ice Age melted. One of the largest is Barkhamsted Reservoir in the north.

ROCKS

Glaciers also sculpted the earth to form ridges and polished layers of rocks. Connecticut's soil is filled with rocks, some of which date back about 400 million years. Sandstone and shale abound in the Connecticut River valley. Traprock, which is quite hard, has been used to build roads.

The fertile land surrounding the Connecticut River is dotted with many farms.

Connecticut's largest traprock quarry, one of the longest in the world, was cut into the Metacomet Ridge near New Haven. Clay deposits, employed in making brick, lie in the Quinnipiac and Housatonic valleys. Western Connecticut produces limestone, used to build homes and to grind into plaster for walls. Connecticut supplied granite for the foundation of the Statue of Liberty and brownstone (a dark sandstone) for buildings in New York City and other parts of the nation.

To early farmers, though, these rocks were a backbreaking burden. Day after day, settlers dug rocks from their fields to make room for crops. One eighteenth-century farmer made up this ironic verse about his land in Cornwall, Connecticut: "Nature out of her boundless store threw rocks together and did no more." People began fashioning piles of rocks into stone fences to mark the boundaries of their property and to keep the neighbors' cows away from their ripening corn. Stone walls, both old and new, are still a common—and charming—sight in this New England state.

Connecticut land owners used stones found in their fields to build their fences. By 1871 almost one-third of the fences in Connecticut were made of stone.

LAND AND WATER

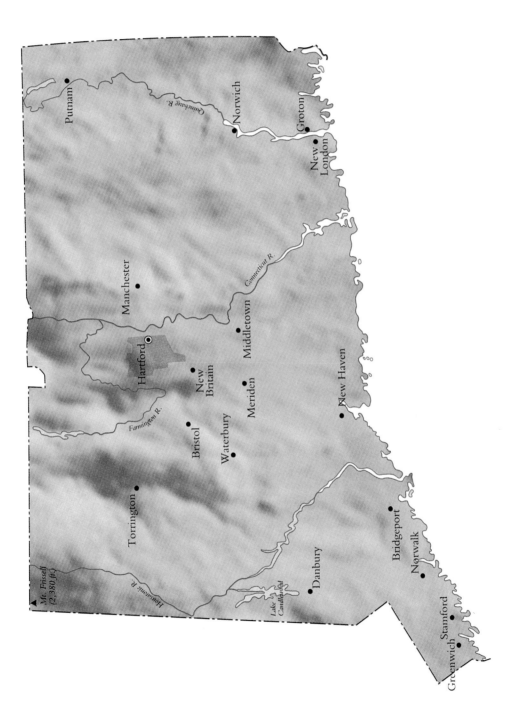

- Putnam
- Norwich
- Groton
- New London
- Quinebaug R.
- Manchester
- Connecticut R.
- Middletown
- Hartford
- New Haven
- New Britain
- Meriden
- Farmington R.
- Bristol
- Waterbury
- Torrington
- Bridgeport
- Norwalk
- Danbury
- Lake Candlewood
- Mt. Frissell (2,380 ft.)
- Housatonic R.
- Stamford
- Greenwich

Connecticut was once almost entirely covered with woods. Today it is still about 60 percent forest, making it one of most heavily wooded states in the United States. Ninety-one state parks cover more than 30,000 acres, and many additional wooded acres are protected from commercial development. One of these is the 840-acre Charles E. Wheeler Wildlife Management Area at the mouth of the Housatonic River where it empties into Long Island Sound. A salt marsh and tidal flats are nearby.

Trees are the centerpiece of Connecticut's magnificent scenery. Dogwoods and other flowering trees mark spring and summer. In the town of Fairfield alone, there are more than 30,000 dogwoods. Brilliant

About 1.8 million acres of forest cover Connecticut.

shades of red, gold, and orange adorn elms, maples, oaks, and other deciduous trees every autumn.

Tapping maple trees for syrup and sugar was common in earlier times and is still done today. In 2005 Connecticut produced 10,000 gallons of maple syrup. During late February and early March, groups of schoolchildren visit farms to see how maple syrup is made. Each fall, visitors to farms throughout the state pay a fee to pick bags of apples for cooking and eating or to buy pumpkins for Halloween.

Various coniferous trees, including pines, cedars, and hemlocks, also abound. December finds many Connecticut families searching tree farms for the perfect holiday tree and greens.

A favorite activity every autumn in Connecticut is pumpkin picking.

A SPELUNKER'S DELIGHT

Spelunkers—people who explore caves—have much to see in Connecticut. The state has more than 275 underground spaces that qualify as caves. Some lie beneath the earth's surface; others can be entered through the sides of hills, cliffs, or mountains.

Inside the caves are interesting lime formations, such as stalactites (which drip from the tops of caves) and stalagmites (which extend up from the floors). Bats, bears, and coyotes make their homes in caves, as do lizards, crayfish, and other creatures. They survive by drinking water that drips into these underground spaces and by eating other living things and their eggs. Fish may also live in caves that contain some water or underground streams.

Over the years, a few legendary people have been known to live in Connecticut's caves. One famous example is a mysterious woman named Sarah Bishop. During the 1800s, Bishop lived for twenty-five years in a cave located near the border of Connecticut and New York State. Bishop viewed the outside world as sinful.

Another hermit, known as The Leatherman, was first spotted in Harwintort, Connecticut, in 1862. For nearly thirty years he wandered along a 365-mile route in central and western Connecticut and eastern New York State. This outdoorsman often slept in caves, and Leatherman Cave in Thomaston, Connecticut, was named after him.

"If you don't like the weather in New England, just wait a minute. It will change," joked the popular author Mark Twain (born Samuel Clemens). Twain, who lived in Connecticut from 1880 to 1910, observed that a rainy day in New England often turned sunny, while a warm, dry day might end with chilly rain.

Parts of New England endure harsh winters, but Connecticut has a humid continental climate, somewhat milder than that of its neighbors. Temperatures rarely rise above ninety-five degrees in the summer or dip below zero in the winter. There are exceptions, however. During the famous blizzard of 1888, for instance, four feet of snow fell within thirty-six hours! Tornadoes and hurricanes are rare, but from spring through fall, storms bring winds that strew leaves and branches across streets and lawns.

Warm summer days can be spent on a beach along the Long Island Sound.

Four distinct seasons mark the year. Autumn's colorful leaves give way to wintry branches dripping with icicles. Frozen ponds beckon to ice-skaters, while snowy hills attract sledders and skiers. Spring is a time of blossoming trees and chattering birds. Summer brings bright flowers to woods and gardens and sunny afternoons at pools, lakes, and beaches.

On average, thirty to thirty-five inches of snow falls along coastal Connecticut, with fifty inches falling in the hills.

PLANTS AND ANIMALS

With a seacoast, many waterways, and forested land within its borders, Connecticut is home to a wide variety of plants and animals. The state is known for its wildflowers, including colorful orchids, pyrola (wintergreen), Indian pipe, and mountain laurel. Cardinal flowers decorate the woods along river valleys.

Millions of years ago dinosaurs roamed the Connecticut River Valley and left behind fossil tracks that intrigue modern-day scientists. Now, smaller animals inhabit the state. People living near wooded areas usually find squirrels, chipmunks, woodchucks, skunks, raccoons, and coyotes in their yard. Motorists on country roads must watch out for deer, wild turkeys, and Canada geese.

Because the land is so diverse, many types of birds live in Connecticut. These include cardinals, whose bright red feathers are a cheerful sight in winter. Warblers, sparrows, thrushes, and robins can be heard singing in many parts of Connecticut. The bald eagle, an endangered bird, still lives in the state. Bird-watchers can see eagles at an observation area located in Southbury and along the Connecticut River during the winter.

Gulls and green herons frequent the beaches of Long Island Sound. Sociable herring gulls approach people in search

The cardinal is a common sight in Connecticut.

Gulls are mostly seen in Connecticut's coastal areas.

of food. They have been known to swoop down on beaches along the sound and snatch the meat right off a picnicker's grill!

Connecticut's waterways have long been a source of fish for food and sport. Along with shellfish found along the coast, trout, bass, carp, and American shad are the most common fish in Connecticut. Shad leave the ocean for the rivers every spring to spawn. During the Revolutionary War, shad, packed in barrels, were fed to the troops. Tons of this fish were also exported to other states and to Europe. New Englanders called shad "poor man's food" because it was so plentiful.

Until the nineteenth century, salmon lived in the Connecticut River, and people caught thousands each year. Newly constructed dams prevented them from reaching their usual spawning grounds. By 1814 the salmon runs had ended. Efforts are under way to restore salmon to Connecticut's tidal rivers.

One unwelcome Connecticut resident is the tick that carries the disease named after the town of Lyme. This bacterial illness was first identified there in 1975. As small as a poppy seed, these ticks live on deer and mice in wooded areas. They can infect both humans and their pets.

Cases of Lyme disease steadily increased during the 1990s. People throughout Connecticut have been warned to protect themselves when they are outdoors during tick season and to check themselves carefully for bites. As of 2005, scientists were still working to develop a safe and effective vaccine to protect people from Lyme disease.

The deer tick, found in the Northeast, including Connecticut, is a transmitter of Lyme disease.

Connecticut is the fourth most densely populated state in the nation, with an estimated 3,510,297 residents as of 2005. As Connecticut's population and industry have grown, so has the demand for more clean water, electric power, and expanded sewage systems. The transportation systems necessary for manufacturing and access to jobs have meant more cars, trains, and trucks. This has led to increased pollution of rivers and streams and the waters of Long Island Sound.

Pollution has long plagued the Connecticut River. The operation of mills and factories sent industrial wastes from ditches and pipes into the water. Dams and dikes, built to prevent flooding, prevented the water from cleansing itself and fertilizing the surrounding land.

People have expressed concern about these problems. As early as 1884, one worried conservationist from Manchester, Connecticut, complained, "A land with its rivers running filth instead of pure water, is like a body with its veins running filth instead of pure blood." During the 1900s citizens, legislators, and business leaders worked together to clean up the Connecticut River, to preserve wildlife, and to save forests and wetlands. Towns improved their sewage treatment plants. Federal pollution laws became stricter during the 1960s and 1970s. Former U.S. senator Abraham Ribicoff, who also served as secretary of health, education, and welfare during the Kennedy administration (1961–1963), led cleanup efforts. He said, "I love the Connecticut [River], not only for what it is but for what we learn about America from it. We must save what is beautiful while there is still time."

In the late 1960s other man-made changes threatened the wildlife in the Connecticut River. Steam generators at nuclear power plants sent heated water into the river and raised its temperature by ten degrees or more. Scientists studied the ways this affected fish.

By the 1990s the Connecticut River was cleaner and people could swim in it again. Parts of the river were designated as national park areas. In 1998 the Connecticut was named one of fourteen American Heritage Rivers in the nation. Under the American Heritage River Initiative, local citizens work with federal agencies to balance environmental and economic concerns while preserving the rivers' historic value.

The Connecticut River Watershed Council works for the protection of New England's largest river, ensuring the survival of its ecosystems and wildlife.

Some fish in Connecticut are endangered, including the shortnose sturgeon, a living fossil that predates the dinosaur. One of the rarest fishes in the United States, it is protected by both federal and state laws. Before the 1800s shortnose sturgeon lived in coastal rivers stretching from Canada to Florida. Today, they live in only sixteen rivers, including the lower half of the Connecticut River. Their numbers declined as a result of overfishing, which began in colonial times, as well as pollution and loss of habitat. Man-made dams also blocked the fish from swimming upstream to their spawning grounds. It is now illegal to keep any shortnose sturgeon found in Connecticut waters. People are asked to report sightings of dead sturgeon to the Department of Environmental Protection's Fisheries Division.

Environmentalists also have focused on protecting the 577 miles of Connecticut and New York coastline that form Long Island Sound. Along the coast, salt water from the ocean mingles with freshwater from rivers and streams. Because of pollution, fish began to die and harbor seals left the area. By the late 1990s, fewer than half the productive shellfish beds in the sound could be harvested. Some beaches were closed to swimmers because of disease-causing organisms in the water.

Keeping Long Island Sound clean is difficult because millions of people live along its coast. Excess nitrogen comes from sewage treatment plants that serve these communities. Nitrogen also comes from the fertilizers people use on their lawns and gardens, some of which reaches coastal waters. Nitrogen causes algae to grow. When the heavy algae plants sink in the water and break down, they consume oxygen that fish and shellfish need to live. Pesticides and toxic wastes from factories also contribute to pollution.

In 1987 the Long Island Sound was designated as a national estuary. Its importance is measured by its beauty and its areas of breeding and nesting for many animals.

In 1994 federal and state agencies joined with universities, environmental agencies, businesses, and the public to form the Comprehensive Conservation and Management Plan for Long Island Sound. Congress approved a $1.5 billion Clear Water/Clean Air Act that provided $200 million for cleanup efforts. By 2000 about $80 million had been used to enlarge and update six sewage treatment plants and to fund nitrogen-removal projects. Money also was allocated for restoring specific animal habitats. New measures were passed to control chemical discharges from boats.

The natural habitat for Connecticut's least shrew is coastal areas. The development of these areas are the greatest threat to this endangered animal.

Long Island Sound still faces many problems in the twenty-first century, however. Conservationists expressed concern in 2004 after President George W. Bush asked Congress for a 90 percent reduction in funding for sound cleanup efforts. Terry Backer, Long Island Soundkeeper and director of the Soundkeeper Fund, said, "Fishable and swimable, that's what our waters should be. That is what our birthright is, a healthy, useable aquatic environment, and what the law requires it to be."

On land, environmentalists work to protect endangered wildlife, such as the least shrew, one of the smallest of all living mammals. These shrews, which resemble moles, live in coastal and southwestern Connecticut. They build burrows or nests and may share a home during nesting season or during the winter. Their numbers declined as coastal lands were developed, and the shrews lost much of their available habitat in coastal marshes and dunes. The least shrew was the first mammal to be listed under Connecticut's Endangered Species Act. To protect them, people are working to prevent further destruction of their habitat.

Chapter Two
A History of Resourcefulness

People in Connecticut have used the land, along with hard work and ingenuity, to survive and thrive. For thousands of years before European settlers arrived, woodland Indians of the Algonkin tribe lived in present-day Connecticut. Historians estimate that these Native Americans numbered about 6,000 to 10,000 in the year 1600. The Pequot were the major tribe, having conquered most of the Connecticut River valley during the 1500s. They controlled about half of the land area that became Connecticut. This group lived mostly in the southeast, along with the Mohegans, an early offshoot of the Pequot tribe. Other tribes included the Narragansett, Nehantic, Paugussett, Wampanoag, and Nipmuc—"Fresh Water People"—who lived near lakes, rivers, and swamps away from the coast.

Native Americans lived along Connecticut's coast as well as in the fertile regions alongside the Connecticut River. They called the region Quinatucquet, *meaning "beside the long tidal river." This painting,* The Connecticut Valley, *was created by Thomas Chambers.*

Groups of Native Americans lived mostly along the coast and in the more fertile river valleys. They built wigwams and longhouses by covering sapling frames with bark, branches, and reeds. Most of their food supply came from hunting and fishing. Using arrowheads crafted from stone, the men caught moose, deer, and bears in the forests, along with wild turkeys and smaller fowl. They caught fish in the rivers and lakes with spears and nets. Coastal tribes also ate shellfish. A smaller part of the Indians' diet came from raising corn, beans, pumpkins, and squash and gathering wild nuts and fruits, including walnuts, chestnuts, butternuts, hazelnuts, acorns, wild cherries, currants, plums, strawberries, blackberries, raspberries, dewberries, blueberries, mulberries, and cranberries. Women did most of the farming, and they wove baskets to hold food and other items.

EARLY SETTLERS

The first white settlement in Connecticut was a trading post. In 1614 Dutch explorer Adriaen Block sailed up the Connecticut River, which he and his crew called the "Fresh River." Long Island Sound was not too deep, and it opened to the sea on the east. This pleased the Dutch, who were interested mostly in trade.

In 1633 Dutch settlers built the House of Good Hope trading post on the river near present-day Hartford and traded with Native Americans for beaver pelts. In that same year, English settlers founded the present-day city Windsor. More English and Dutch settlers followed.

Relations between whites and Indians became less friendly during the 1630s. The Europeans brought into the region unfamiliar diseases such as smallpox. Thousands of Indians died because they had not developed resistance to these diseases. Conflicts with the Pequots turned violent over land disputes in 1637. The colonists, with their metal armor, muskets, and swords, quickly defeated the Indians in the Pequot War. English soldiers killed an estimated six hundred men, women, and children in the Indian village of Mystic by setting its seventy wigwams on fire.

During the 1630s, English settlers in Massachusetts began to move into the Connecticut River valley. The Pequot War cleared the way for the expansion and destroyed the powerful Pequots.

In 1638 New Haven was founded by the Reverend John Davenport and Thomas Eaten and their followers. About 250 Puritans from Boston paid the Indians for this land with twenty-four knives, twenty-three coats, twelve spoons, twelve hatchets, and some scissors and garden hoes. The New Haven government was based on a set of laws called the Fundamental Agreement. The Bible was the supreme law for the colony. The Puritans banned long hair on men and all fancy clothing. On Sunday, people could only leave home to attend church or religious meetings. People who broke certain laws could be severely punished, even put to death. Only Puritan church members could vote or hold office.

A DOCUMENT FOR FREEDOM

In 1639 residents of Wethersfield, Windsor, and Hartford formed the Colony of Connecticut. Unlike the New Haven colony, their government was based on a remarkable document inspired by Reverend Thomas Hooker. In 1636 Hooker had brought a group of colonists from Massachusetts to found the settlement that became Hartford. Hooker wanted to develop a settlement based on what he called "a true government of the people." He said that citizens should be able to choose their own leaders, who would then have to account for their actions.

People discussed Hooker's ideas, and a large group of colonists approved laws called the Fundamental Orders on January 14, 1639. This was the first document in the United States to say that a government gets its power from "the free consent of the people." It gave Connecticut one of its nicknames, the Constitution State.

In later years, the Fundamental Orders inspired others, including Thomas Jefferson, who wrote much of the Declaration of Independence, and James Madison, who wrote a great deal of both the U.S. Constitution and the Bill of Rights.

In order to gain religious freedom, the Reverend Thomas Hooker and one hundred followers left England for the New World where they established a new settlement, now known as Hartford.

THE CHARTER OAK

In 1661 John Winthrop Jr., the sixth governor of the Colony of Connecticut, visited King Charles II of England with an unusual request: would the king recognize the colony's form of government? The king agreed and granted the colony a charter that permitted self-rule the next year.

After Charles died in 1685, his brother, King James II, revoked this charter. In 1686 James named his friend Edmund Andros governor of the Dominion of New England, an area that included Connecticut. Andros traveled to Hartford in October 1687 and demanded that Governor Robert Treat give him the charter. One evening a big meeting was held by the light of many candles. Just as the charter was brought out and shown to Andros, the candles suddenly went out. Colonists smuggled the charter out a window and hid it inside the hollow of a nearby oak tree. Andros was forced to

leave empty-handed. Still, he declared that the charter was invalid and assumed control over Connecticut, which he annexed to Massachusetts. Andros lost his authority in 1688 when King James II was overthrown.

The tree that protected the charter became known as the Charter Oak. It was cherished as a monument until an ice storm destroyed it in 1856. A special marker shows where the tree once stood.

More settlers arrived in Connecticut during the late 1600s. Relations between Native Americans and whites were mostly peaceful, but some colonists were affected by King Philip's War, a Native American uprising that took place in 1675 and 1676. King Philip, a Wampanoag chief, led tribes who were upset by the expanding white settlements. They attacked white communities along the Connecticut River, mostly in Massachusetts. Soldiers from Connecticut joined other colonists fighting the Indians. In March 1676 warriors attacked Simsbury and burned it to the ground.

As the 1700s began, trade flourished. Colonists grew corn, rye, barley, peas, and wheat. They raised sheep and cows and made cloth from wool and a plant called flax. Using animal fat and ashes gathered from their fireplaces, they made soap every spring. Children often had to stir the soap as it bubbled in a large kettle over an outdoor fire.

Young people also worked in the fields growing and harvesting crops. While planting corn seeds children often sang this old rhyme:

One for the bug,
One for the crow,
One to rot,
And two to grow.

In 1650 the colony passed a law requiring every town with more than fifty families to run an elementary school. Towns with more than one hundred families had to maintain a secondary school, too. In these one-room schools, one teacher helped students of all ages. Schools had few books.

During the 1700s life in Connecticut was one of hard work that included planting and harvesting crops.

Children learned to read by using a slate or a hornbook with the alphabet written on one side. They recited their lessons aloud and had regular spelling contests. Today, visitors to the Little Red Schoolhouse in Simsbury and similar buildings in other towns can see these colonial schools.

The founders of New Haven dreamed of a fine college to educate their leaders. The town could not afford one, however. In 1700 Reverend John Pierpont organized a group to collect funds for a new college, which was founded in Killingworth in 1701. Ten clergymen were the first trustees. By 1716 a permanent building was completed in New Haven, where the college was relocated.

At 216 feet tall Harkness Tower is a notable feature of Yale University.

Elihu Yale, who once had lived in Boston, sent books to the new college from England, where his family lived. Yale also sent shipments of goods, which the trustees could sell to raise funds for the school. The college, which the trustees named Yale in his honor, is now considered one of the finest universities in the world.

A visitor in the early 1700s noted Connecticut's "numerous towns, villages, and hamlets, almost everywhere exhibiting marks of prosperity and improvement; the rare appearance of decline; the numerous churches lifting their spires . . . , the neat school houses, every where occupied; and the mills, busied on such a multitude of streams. It may be safely asserted, that a pleasanter journey will rarely be found than that, which is made in the Connecticut Valley."

As Connecticut grew and prospered, many towns were established. Roadways were built linking them together.

By the late 1700s people from France, Scotland, and Ireland had joined English and Dutch settlers in the colony, where they often worked as farmers and as fishermen. A child walking the streets of Hartford would pass the shops of carpenters, tanners, shoemakers, coopers, blacksmiths, and tailors. Windows displayed hats, cabinets, jewelry, silver, candles, and clocks.

Some of the homes built by colonists still stand today. Built around 1639, the Whitfield House in Guilford is the oldest house in Connecticut and perhaps the oldest stone house in New England. Buttolph-Williams House in Wethersfield was one of the finest houses in the area during the 1600s. The kitchen has a large collection of original furnishings. Elegant Elmwood in Windsor, built in 1740, contains a tapestry given to the family by the French emperor Napoleon. Restored houses in Greenwich date back to the early 1700s. The Bush-Holley House sponsors History Week each year, and children can try their hand at colonial chores such as baking, sewing, and sheep-shearing.

FIGHTING FOR FREEDOM

Connecticut played an active role when the colonies fought against the British to become an independent nation. During the Revolutionary War, from 1775 to 1783, Connecticut sent more soldiers (in relation to its population) than any other colony. About 30,000 men from the colony served in the army, second in number only to Massachusetts, which had a larger population.

General George Washington called Connecticut the Provisions State because it sent so many supplies to the army. In 1777 Hartford sent $30,000 to buy supplies for Washington's troops. The following year, during the harsh winter of 1777–1778 at Valley Forge, Pennsylvania,

Governor Jonathan Trumbull shipped the revolutionary troops thousands of barrels of pork and beef by ox sled. Powder mills at Westville and New Haven supplied much-needed gunpowder.

Connecticut also helped to lead the Americans to victory at sea. The colony's small navy captured more than forty British vessels. The first American submarine, a one-person vessel called the *Turtle*, was

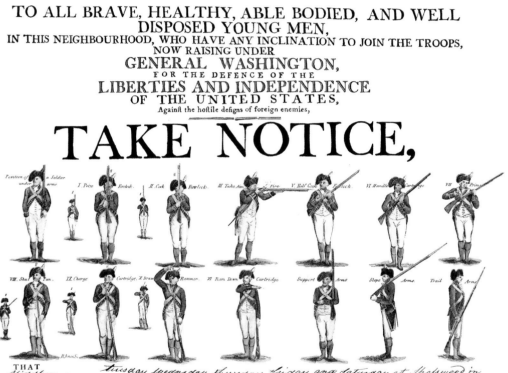

During the Revolutionary War recruiting posters were created to entice men to join the army.

built by David Bushnell of Saybrook, Connecticut, in 1776. The craft failed to blow up a British ship in New York Harbor as planned, but submarines played a key role in future wars. A replica of the *Turtle* is on permanent display at the Connecticut River Museum in Essex, Connecticut. A second replica of the *Turtle* is on display at the U.S. Navy Submarine Force Museum in Groton, Connecticut.

In 1782 General George Washington created a medal for bravery in battle. He called it the Purple Heart. The first three men to receive it were from Connecticut. Washington cited them for their "daring" and "unusual gallantry" in battle. There is a Purple Heart Museum in Enfield, Connecticut.

In all, about three hundred African-American soldiers from Connecticut served in the Colonial Army. Lemuel Haynes of West Hartford fought at the Battle of Concord. After the war, he became a prominent Congregationalist minister, poet, and essayist. Jordan Freeman gave his life at Fort Griswold. He attacked a British soldier who had just killed his commander, Colonel Ledyard, after Ledyard surrendered. British soldiers killed Freeman and the other Americans at the fort in a raid planned by Benedict Arnold, a Connecticut war hero turned traitor. Freeman's bravery is commemorated with a memorial plaque at Fort Griswold.

AFRICAN AMERICANS

By the mid-1700s about three to five thousand African Americans, most of them slaves, were living in Connecticut. There were no large plantations to make slavery as profitable as it was in the South, yet there were a few colonists who owned numerous slaves. Most slaves in New England worked as house servants, farmers, shoemakers, wagon drivers, or barbers.

In the North, many African Americans worked as household slaves.

The few African Americans who were free had no political rights and were subject to the "black codes," enacted in the late 1600s. These codes required free blacks to pay taxes but banned them from voting, holding public office, and serving on a jury. Free blacks formed a separate society and elected their own governor, but the black governor had no political power.

By the 1700s a growing number of white citizens opposed slavery. A 1774 law banned bringing new slaves into the colony.

After the Revolutionary War, slaves who had been soldiers were freed. The Connecticut Emancipation Law, enacted in 1784, said that any child born to slaves would be free at age twenty-five. By 1800, 80 percent of all blacks in the state were free. Slavery officially ended in the state in 1848.

A dramatic incident involving slavery touched Connecticut in 1839. A group of captive Africans, many of them from the Mende people, were en route to Cuba on the Spanish-owned slave ship *Amistad*. On July 1, they rebelled and killed several crew members. They told the slave traders to take them back to Africa, but instead, the Spaniards headed toward North America.

In August the *Amistad* approached Long Island, where it was seized and taken to New London, Connecticut. Joseph Cinque (also known as Singbe-Pieh), leader of the mutiny, and his fellow Africans were accused of murder and piracy and taken to New Haven. They were put on trial in Hartford, Connecticut. To defend them, abolitionists—people who opposed slavery—hired well-known lawyers to take their case. These lawyers argued that the Africans were kidnap victims, not slaves, when they rebelled.

In January 1840 Judge Andrew Judson ruled in favor of the Africans. He declared that they had been "born free, and ever since have been and still of right are free and not slaves." Their mutiny was a desperate act of self-defense.

The decision was appealed and reached the U.S. Supreme Court in 1841. Although five of the justices were southerners who owned slaves, they agreed with Judson's decision. The Africans were allowed to return home. A replica of the *Amistad*, built at the Mystic Seaport in Mystic, Connecticut, is winter-ported there.

THE BATTLE OF STONINGTON

During the War of 1812, the United States fought Britain in what has been called the Second War of Independence. Britain was at war with France, and the British navy was blocking trade between the French and the Americans. The British blockaded American ports and seized thousands of American seamen to work on their ships. The war hindered Connecticut's shipping industry and international trade. Britain was winning the war in August 1814 when their troops attacked Stonington, Connecticut. The people of Stonington defended their town, and their success boosted American morale. The war ended in 1814.

By Philip Freneau

Three gal-lant ships from Eng-land came, Freight-ed deep with fire and flame, And oth-er things we need not name, To have a dash at Ston-ing-ton. Now safe ar-rived, they work be-gun; they tho't to make the Yank-ees run, And

have a might-y deal of fun, In— steal-ing sheep at Ston - ing - ton.

The *Ramilies* first began the attack,
And *Nimrod* made a mighty crack,
And none can tell what kept them back
From setting fire to Stonington.
Their bombs were thrown, their rockets
    flew,
And not a man of all their crew,
Though every man stood full in view,
Could kill a man of Stonington.

To have a turn we thought but fair.
We Yankees brought two guns to bear,
And, sir, it would have made you stare
To have seen the smoke at Stonington.
We bored the *Nimrod* through and
    through.
And killed and mangled half her crew,
When, riddled, crippled, she withdrew
And cursed the boys of Stonington.

They killed a goose, they killed a hen,
Three hogs they wounded in a pen;
They dashed away—and pray, what
    then?
That was not taking Stonington.
The shells were thrown, the rockets flew,
But not a shell of all they threw,
Though every house was in full view,
Could burn a house in Stonington.

The *Ramilies* then gave up the fray,
And with her comrades sneaked away;
Such was the valor on that day
Of British tars at Stonington.
Now, some assart on sartin grounds,
Beside their damage and their wounds,
It cost the king ten thousand pounds
To have a fling at Stonington.

POPULATION GROWTH: 1720–2000

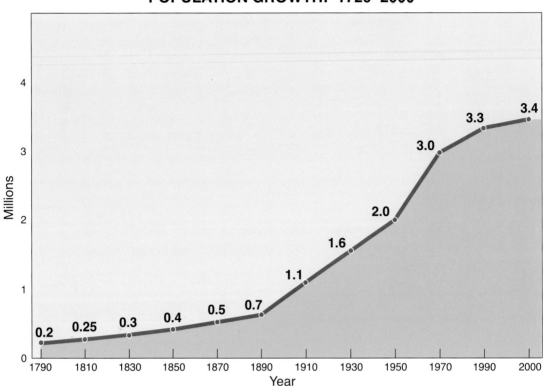

GROWTH OF A STATE

Connecticut became the fifth state in the union on January 9, 1788, when residents approved the United States Constitution.

State Senator Roger Sherman, who helped write the Declaration of Independence, also contributed to the Constitution. He and Oliver Ellsworth and William Samuel Johnson proposed the "Connecticut Compromise," which allowed each state to elect the same number of senators (two) to the U.S. Congress while sending different numbers of representatives to the House of Representatives based on the state's population.

The early 1800s saw steady economic growth. Factories produced furniture, cotton thread, woolen cloth, and paper, among other things. Describing the changing terrain in 1804, geographer and clergyman Jedidiah Morse wrote, "The state is checkered with innumerable roads or highways crossing each other in every direction. A traveler in any of these roads, even in the most unsettled parts of the state, will seldom pass more than half a mile or a mile without finding a house, or a farm. . . ."

After 1800 steamboats became an important means of transportation for both business and pleasure. Visitors traveled up the Connecticut River to visit resort hotels and summer theaters. Later in the century, Connecticut's railway system, used for transporting goods and passengers, became the most dense in the nation.

"Yankee ingenuity" spurred manufacturing. Samuel Colt of Hartford made the first repeating pistol, the six-shooter, which was patented in 1836. Colt opened a factory to produce these guns, which were used widely on the western frontier.

During the 1800s, steamboats traveled from New York City to Hartford on a regular schedule and steam trains traveled through the city carrying passengers and goods.

CONNECTICUT YANKEE PEDDLERS

During the 1700s most people in Connecticut lived on farms. They looked forward to a visit from traveling peddlers who brought horse carts filled with cloth, scissors, combs, hats, and cookware to their homes. As one observer noted, "Shining coffee pots were crammed with spools of thread, papers of pins, cards of horn buttons, and cakes of shaving soap—and bolts of gaudy [ribbon] could be drawn from the pepper-boxes and sausage-stuffers."

"Connecticut Yankee peddlers," as they were called, had a reputation as clever traders. Colonial housewives liked to flavor their dishes with nutmeg, an imported spice. Some shady peddlers carved small, hard wooden "nutmegs" and sold them to customers, who later discovered the trick. Old stories about wooden nutmegs gave Connecticut its most amusing nickname, the Nutmeg State.

Old tales about these tricky peddlers abound. In one story, a Yankee peddler is riding with some folks on a stagecoach out west. One passenger tells the others, "We're nearing Camden, the last stop."

"Glad to hear it," said the peddler. "I'm hungry as a dog."

"Too bad," the man tells him. "You'll get only a few mouthfuls before the stagecoach comes back for us. If you try to finish eating, you'll lose your seat."

The Yankee just grins. "I'll bet you a free supper that I finish my meal and still keep my seat."

Once in Camden, the passengers hurry to the inn. The innkeeper charges fifty cents apiece for supper, but they are too hungry to fuss. They no sooner start eating when the innkeeper calls out, "Stagecoach is here! Driver won't wait but a minute."

Everyone rushes out, all but the Yankee. He keeps on eating and even asks for some bread pudding.

"You'll lose your seat," warns the innkeeper.

The Yankee shrugs and asks for a spoon.

"There's plenty on the table—real silver, too," the man replies.

"Hmm," says the Yankee, looking all around. "You don't suppose those folks took off with 'em, seeing as they paid so much money for only a few bites of supper?"

"Thunderation!" cries the innkeeper and storms outside.

The Yankee finishes eating, then walks outside. A big, noisy crowd has gathered near the stagecoach, and the Camden sheriff is standing beside the passengers. The sheriff approaches the Yankee and says, "Kindly point out the thieves."

The peddler scratches his chin and looks at the innkeeper. "Seems I was mistaken," he says. "If you go look in your coffeepot, you'll find all your spoons. And thanks for a mighty fine meal!"

And that's how one clever Yankee outwitted an innkeeper who liked to charge folks for food they didn't have time to eat.

In 1794 Connecticut native Eli Whitney perfected the cotton gin. Cotton crops became much more profitable once people could use gins to remove the seeds faster. This led to the increased use of slaves for farming cotton in the South and the development of more textile mills in both North and South.

Whitney also started a gun factory in present-day Hamden, Connecticut. His machines were among the first to make identical parts. When a part broke, a customer could replace it instead of waiting for someone to make the part by hand. The introduction of assembly lines, tried by both Whitney and Colt, led to modern methods of mass production that made goods cheaper to manufacture.

In 1839 Charles Goodyear of Naugatuck found a way to strengthen rubber through a process called vulcanization. In Stamford, Linus Yale invented the first modern lock in 1848. Other factories made brass, lace, tools, and sewing machines. The first bicycle made in the United States came from Connecticut, and the state became known for its fine clocks after Eli Terry set up a factory in Plymouth in 1804.

Today you can see both these early timepieces and later ones at the famous American Clock and Watch Museum in Bristol's Miles Lewis House. More than three thousand clocks made after 1790 are on display. Along with plain wooden ones, there are clocks with nursery rhyme characters, cartoon favorites, and animals. One grandfather clock is a towering ten feet tall.

In towns and cities near the sea, shipbuilding became a key industry. Sailors in search of whale oil set out from these ports. The largest fleets sailed from Mystic, Stonington, and New London. By 1860 many of the whales had been killed, and petroleum began to replace whale oil for use in lamps. By 1889 only three whaling vessels remained in the state.

Sealing was also important. A Stonington native, Nathaniel Palmer, sailed with a sealing expedition to the South Atlantic in 1820 looking for new sealeries. He discovered the Antarctic Peninsula.

A nineteenth-century whaling village has been re-created at Mystic Seaport beside the Mystic River. In the harbor you can climb aboard the whaling vessel *Charles W. Morgan* for a closer look at the decks and cabins. Visitors can also put on wigs, hats, aprons, or eye patches and play the part of sea captains, crew members, pirates, or sailors' wives in outdoor plays.

PART OF THE UNION ARMY

During the Civil War Connecticut sent into battle 57,379 recruits, which may have amounted to about half the young men in the state. This was five times more than the Union Army had expected from such a small state. These men fought at Bull Run, Gettysburg, and Antietam as well as many other battles. More than 20,000 died, were wounded, or were missing in action.

General Ulysses S. Grant was surrounded by an honor guard made up of the First Connecticut Volunteers when he accepted the surrender of General Robert E. Lee of the Confederate Army. The first Union soldiers to reach Richmond, Virginia, when it fell in 1865 were the all-black Twenty-ninth Regiment from Connecticut.

INTO THE TWENTIETH CENTURY

By 1900 Connecticut had in many ways left behind its Puritan origins and farming ways. Immigrants had come from all over Europe, including the Irish who left during the potato famines of the mid-1800s. People arrived from Scandinavia and Germany, then from the Mediterranean and Central and Eastern Europe. They sought economic opportunity and political and religious freedom.

Over the years immigrants moved inland from the coast and to manufacturing towns with waterpower, harbors, and rail systems. The largest of these were New Haven, Bridgeport, Danbury, Waterbury, New Britain, Hartford, and Norwich. By 1900, ten towns produced two-thirds of all the state's manufacturing and were home to about half of the state's residents. By 1910 first-generation immigrants made up 30 percent of Connecticut's population.

During World War I, men and women from Connecticut again served in the military. Factories in the state made hundreds of thousands of pistols, rifles, bayonets, and other military supplies. By the last year of the war, 80 percent of the state's factories were involved in the defense industry.

Since its economy relied on industry, Connecticut was hit hard by the Great Depression of the 1930s. World War II boosted the economy. Workers made airplanes, guns, submarines, and helicopters for England and France, which began fighting Germany in 1939. The demand soared after the United States entered the war in December 1941. Connecticut produced more war goods per person than any other state.

World War II aircraft were built in Bridgeport, employing over 500,000 people by 1944.

After the war, in the late 1940s, more than half of the state's workers had factory jobs. The economy had changed with the times. Defense-industry jobs decreased in the late 1980s when political changes lowered the demand for military weapons. As a result, electronics, machine tools, and service-oriented businesses, such as insurance, became more important. The state is also known for its many small and medium-sized businesses.

NEW CHALLENGES

Connecticut continues to face social, economic, and political challenges in the twenty-first century, including the threat of terrorism. People in the state were strongly affected by the attacks that destroyed the World Trade Center in New York City on September 11, 2001. Seventy-two Connecticut residents died that day, and others were injured. Many residents knew one or more of the victims or had worked in the stricken area. Connecticut state troopers and members of the National Guard have been providing added security on commuter trains that transport thousands of people to and from their jobs inside Connecticut and between Connecticut and New York.

Connecticut towns near the New York border have prepared themselves for the possibility of a mass evacuation if New York is attacked again. To deal with terrorist threats, police and fire departments improved their communication systems and acquired new equipment, such as protective suits and decontamination trailers. Some Connecticut police receive special training in dealing with suicide bombers. In 2004 John Buturla, the state's acting homeland security director, said, "In the past three years, we've made strides in improving the level of preparedness."

Chapter Three

Living in the Nutmeg State

People from many walks of life call Connecticut home. They include actors, television personalities, authors, artists, musicians, and corporate executives as well as "everyday" people. One Southport resident said, "At the beach this summer, I saw a radio talk-show host, a former tennis champion, several actors and musicians, and an award-winning playwright."

Throughout its history, Connecticut has relied on the energy and creativity of its people. Whether they worked on farms or in factories, businesses, education, government, or other settings, people have built the state. As educator Homer Babbage noted in 1978, "A tiny little state, devoid of natural resources, has compiled a record of human resourcefulness that [deserves] the admiration of all."

People of many cultures call Connecticut home. They enjoy the history and heritage of the state.

The people of Connecticut come from around the world. After the 1600s the next large wave of immigrants arrived in the 1800s. By 1860 Irish immigrants numbered about 55,000, making them the largest immigrant group in Connecticut.

As time went on, more people came from eastern and southern Europe. By 1910, 55 percent of Connecticut's immigrants came from these regions, most of them from Italy. With a total of 59,954 people, Italians had become the second-largest immigrant group after the Irish.

Students at Hooker Elementary School celebrate the cultural diversity of Connecticut during International Day festivities.

Like the people who came before them, these new Americans made their way in Connecticut by finding jobs in factories, stone quarries, and agricultural industries or starting businesses. Through hard work and education, many improved their lives and those of their descendants. One man from Fairfield County described his family's experience this way: "My grandfather worked as a mason for this building company when he came to America from Italy. Now, my brothers and I, we own it."

Although Connecticut gradually became more diverse, the state remained mostly white. The 1960 U.S. Census showed that the state's residents included fewer than one thousand Native Americans and about 110,000 African Americans. By 2004 African Americans made up about 9.3 percent of the population, while people of Hispanic or Latino descent accounted for 10.6 percent. About 0.2 percent were Native Americans.

In recent years, more immigrants have come from Asia, Africa, South America, the Caribbean, and Eastern Europe. People of Asian descent come mostly from Cambodia, China, India, Indonesia, and Japan, Korea, Pakistan, Thailand, Vietnam, and the Philippines made up about 3 percent of the population in 2004.

The Hispanic population in Connecticut is one of the fastest growing in the state.

A higher-than-average percentage of Asian students attend college, including the University of Connecticut in Storrs. In 1997 the university opened its Asian American Cultural Center in order to aid Asian American students and to help others to understand and appreciate Asian culture. People can enjoy art, music, and literature through cultural displays, performances, and social events at the center.

Hungarians make up the largest group from central-eastern Europe. Most of these people of Hungarian descent live in Fairfield County. The number of Hungarian Americans in Bridge-

Over the ten year period of 1990–2000, the Asian community in Connecticut grew 63 percent.

port and its suburbs is second only to Cleveland, Ohio. Some arrived after the Soviet Union invaded Hungary after World War II and then crushed an anti-Soviet uprising in 1956. Others immigrated after 1989 to escape the crime and unemployment that rose after Soviet domination ended.

By the 1980s about 80 percent of the population, more than 2.5 million people, lived in urban areas. Many of these families originally came from other countries or states to work in factories or in Connecticut's defense industry when those jobs were plentiful. By 2004 more than 3 million people lived in Connecticut's urban regions.

ETHNIC CONNECTICUT

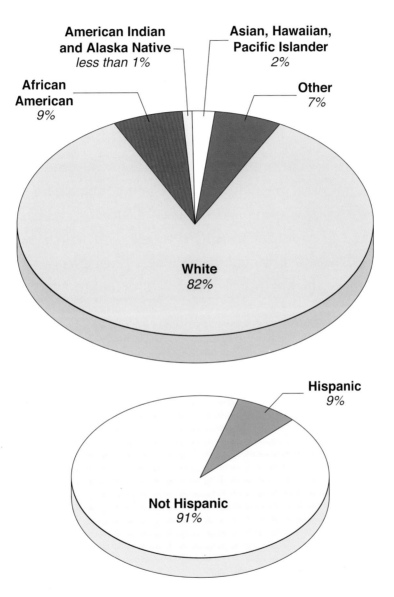

American Indian
and Alaska Native
less than 1%

Asian, Hawaiian,
Pacific Islander
2%

African
American
9%

Other
7%

White
82%

Hispanic
9%

Not Hispanic
91%

*Note: A person of Cuban, Mexican, Puerto Rican, South or Central American,
or other Spanish culture or origin, regardless of race, is defined as Hispanic.*

TWO CONNECTICUTS

The per capita income of Connecticut—around $45,506 a year in 2004—is the highest in the nation. Average incomes in some communities are well above $50,000, and an average three- or four-bedroom home may cost more than half a million dollars. In Bridgeport, New Haven, Hartford, and certain other cities, incomes are much lower and crime rates and unemployment are higher. That is why some observers say that there are two Connecticuts.

There are strong contrasts between the lifestyle of people in small towns and cities. The Gold Coast—Greenwich and other wealthy towns along Long Island Sound—is the location of many fine homes, some of them large estates, set on landscaped grounds. There are golf courses, tennis and hunt clubs, polo and croquet games, and marinas filled with yachts and boats. Stage, screen, and television personalities mingle with writers, artists, athletes, business executives, and publishers. Some affluent residents use these Gold Coast homes, which may cost millions of dollars, only as summer or weekend retreats.

Summer homes of Connecticut's Gold Coast face the Long Island Sound.

POPULATION DENSITY

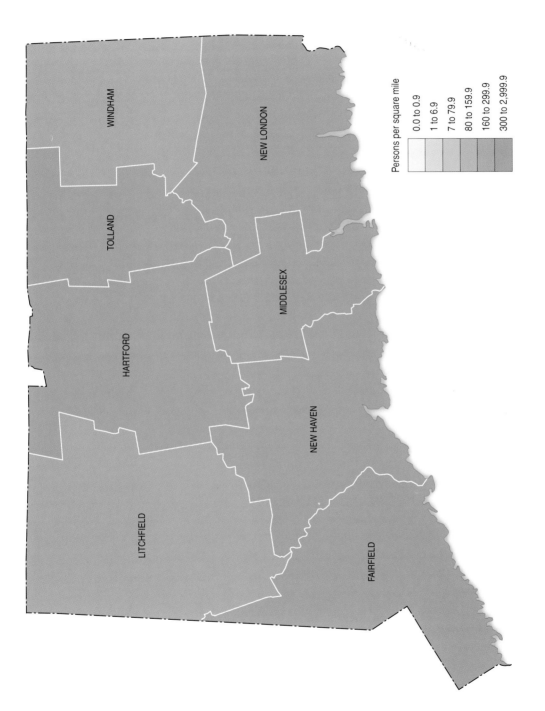

Persons per square mile

0.0 to 0.9
1 to 6.9
7 to 79.9
80 to 159.9
160 to 299.9
300 to 2,999.9

WINDHAM

NEW LONDON

TOLLAND

MIDDLESEX

HARTFORD

NEW HAVEN

LITCHFIELD

FAIRFIELD

Celebrities and other wealthy people also buy homes in the quiet, northwest part of the state, called Litchfield Hills, as private retreats from New York City or Los Angeles. Steeped in New England tradition, this region features old churches and village greens, colonial and Victorian buildings, and wooded areas.

Most of the communities in Connecticut are classified as towns, many with populations around 20,000 or less. Larger cities are far more crowded. Suburban areas near large cities may house upper- or middle-class citizens, while the inner cities are plagued with run-down dwellings and housing projects.

Many families live far below the poverty line. Although the poverty rate in the state as a whole (8 percent in 2003) is lower than the national average, it is concentrated in the cities. The rates of childhood poverty in Bridgeport, Hartford, and New Haven are among the highest in the nation. This is a source of ongoing concern to many people in the state. Most of the poorer citizens in Connecticut are minorities, which means that large cities in the state are both racially and economically different from smaller towns. The white population in small towns is about 95 percent, while in urban areas it is 80.5 percent.

COPING WITH CRIME

Statistics show that crime rates in Connecticut are lower than the national average. However, crime rates are above the national average in cities that suffer from high rates of poverty and unemployment. Many crimes in the state are connected with illegal drugs, and an increasing number involve young people.

In some small towns, a murder may occur only once in a decade, if that often. The murder rate in Bridgeport is more than four times the national average and, at one time, the city had the highest per capita murder rate in the nation. In Hartford, the number of shootings reached ninety during the first six months of 2005. More than half of these shootings took place in the same three neighborhoods in one section of the city. To combat these crimes, more police began patrolling the streets.

Like many other states, Connecticut has set longer terms for convicted criminals with less chance for parole. The state also enforces harsher penalties for repeat offenders. Connecticut has a death penalty, and ten men were on death row as of 2005. Convicted serial killer Michael Ross was executed in 2005. State correctional facilities have developed self-help programs for inmates who seek counseling, education, and job training.

In order to protect Connecticut's communities from rising incidents of crime, more police officers have been assigned to safeguard the streets.

RELIGIOUS BELIEFS

Although it began as a colony led by Puritan-Congregationalist clergymen, Connecticut gradually became more open to other beliefs. In 1818 a new constitution included a law that forced everyone to pay taxes to the Congregationalist Church. The church no longer controlls politics in the state.

Despite the strong Congregational influence, people of other faiths arrived during the colonial period. Jewish citizens have lived in Connecticut since the Revolutionary War. Scandinavian and German immigrants brought their diverse Protestant traditions.

In the nineteenth century Irish Catholic immigrants faced discrimination because of their nationality and religion. Anti-Catholic demonstrations and riots took place around the country. In Hartford, a Catholic church was burned down. Irish citizens worked for acceptance and political change, and some became community leaders. Anti-Catholic sentiments declined, and life became easier for the Italian and Polish Catholic immigrants who came later.

By the twenty-first century Catholics were the largest single religious group in Connecticut. However, there were more Protestants overall, including Congregationalists, Episcopalians, Lutherans, Presbyterians, Baptists, Methodists, Christian Scientists, and Quakers, as well as Unitarians. Asian communities included Christians and Buddhists, Hindus, and Shintos. Muslims also could be found throughout Connecticut.

Connecticut's diverse culture has introduced various religious beliefs throughout the state. This woman prays during a Sikh worship service.

SUCCOTASH FOR SUPPER

Traditional dishes in Connecticut were simple and made use of products that were grown at home or on nearby farms. Cooking was plain but hearty and nourishing. During the early days, corn was the main crop, eaten on the cob, in soups, and in various kinds of bread. These breads were sometimes sweetened with honey or maple syrup. This tasty version of succotash can be made with just a few ingredients.

Creamy Succotash (serves 4–6)
2 cups fresh or frozen lima beans
2 1/2 cups yellow corn kernels
3 tablespoons butter
1 teaspoon sugar
3/4 teaspoon salt
1/4 teaspoon pepper, if desired
3/4 cup heavy cream
(Ask an adult to help you with this.)

1. Cook the beans, covered with boiling salted water, in a saucepan for seven to eight minutes. They should be tender but still firm.

2. Add the corn and cook for five more minutes. Drain the corn and beans and set aside.

3. Melt the butter in a heavy skillet over medium heat. Add the drained corn and beans and stir to coat. Add the other ingredients and stir until they are well blended.

Succotash goes well with sliced tomatoes, biscuits, and baked apples sweetened with maple syrup.

NATIVE AMERICANS

Although Native Americans were once declared "extinct" in Connecticut, several thousand live there today, both on and off reservations. One tiny reservation, about half a block in size, is located in Trumbull. A few Indians also live on the Schaghticoke Reservation in Kent. Two large Pequot reservations were set up in Ledyard and in North Stonington.

Like other tribes in the United States, the Ledyard group has sovereign status and can operate outside state law. In 1983 the Mashantucket Pequots planned a large gambling casino complex called Foxwoods. They agreed to pay the state one-quarter of the annual profits from their slot-machine business. The state uses this money to fund social and education programs in large cities.

Foxwoods includes a large gambling building, three hotels, restaurants, shops, three theaters, and a 1,500-seat showroom for live entertainment. At the turn of the twenty-first century, it was the largest gaming resort in the Western Hemisphere and one of the largest and most profitable casinos in the world. The business brought in more than $1 billion dollars a year and created new jobs in the state, as well as increasing tourism. Local residents complained, however, about increased traffic, speeding, littering, and higher crime rates.

About 1,500 Mohegans live around present-day Norwich and Montville near Fort Shantok State Park. They are one of the largest tribes on the East Coast. Native American historian Virginia DeMarce said that the tribe survived because "they shrewdly learned to cope with the new circumstances." They also seek to preserve their distinct culture and language. Bruce "Two Dogs" Bozsum contributes to this effort as a musician and as the head of the Mohegan Language Restoration Project. As of 2005 Bozsum also serves as tribal council chairman.

To celebrate their heritage, native groups gather at the Native American Dance Festival sponsored by the Mashantucket Pequot tribe.

In 1995 the Mohegans settled a longstanding land dispute with the state of Connecticut. The 138-acre tract of land that includes Fort Shantok was returned to the tribe. The next year they began building a gambling complex. The vast Mohegan Sun casino includes gaming rooms, restaurants, and a 10,000-square-foot nightclub. Profits from this business are used for the welfare of the Mohegans. Everyone has access to tribal health insurance, and all young people can attend vocational school or college, paid for by the tribe, if they maintain a B+ average.

The Mohegan Sun casino is owned and operated by the Mohegan tribe.

RICH TRADITIONS

People from different cultures have contributed their talents and traditions to life in Connecticut. During the summer of 2005 people in south-eastern Connecticut could attend events featuring Japanese folk dancing and various kinds of music—Latin salsa, classical piano, blues, swing, jazz, rap, pop, and bluegrass.

Based in Connecticut, the Salt and Pepper Gospel Singers is an interracial group that includes people of different religions. It was founded in 1985 with forty members. They perform throughout Connecticut at churches, homeless shelters, prisons, colleges, weddings, and community events, and they have appeared at music festivals and in concert halls around the nation.

In Connecticut national holidays are often marked by traditional New England costumes and ceremonies, some with fifes and drums. Towns may re-create events from their history, such as Revolutionary War battles, on the Fourth of July.

A Civil War reenactment authenticates a battle scene between the Confederate and Union armies.

Ethnic restaurants can be found around the state, and people share favorite dishes at food festivals. To the traditional New England cornbreads, baked beans, meats, and seafood, new dishes have been added from a variety of cultures such as Irish, Italian, Mexican, Chinese, Japanese, Thai, Hungarian, Bulgarian, Brazilian, Portuguese, Jamaican, and Puerto Rican.

YEAR-ROUND ACTIVITIES

Connecticut does not have a state fair, but regional fairs, festivals, and cultural events abound. There are art shows, street fairs, flea markets, sailing contests, and international food fairs.

Italians are the largest ethnic group in the state, and summer is a time for Festival Italiano in many towns. The Sons of Italy sponsor these events to raise money for charities. One teenager who goes to the local festival each year with her family now helps her father to sell pizza in one of the booths. She said, "It's a fun part of summer I just wouldn't miss."

The state is a center for equestrian sports, with more horses per square mile than any other state. Well-known hunt and riding clubs operate here, and horse shows draw riders from around the nation. Several Olympic equestrians, including Leslie Burr Howard of Westport, learned the sport while growing up in Connecticut. Howard was a member of the team that won a gold medal at the 1984 Olympics and a silver medal at the 1996 Olympics. Another Westporter, William Steinkraus, won the individual gold medal for show jumping in 1968. He was the first American to win an Olympic gold medal in show jumping.

Snowmobiling, sledding, and downhill and cross-country skiing are favorite winter sports. From 1972 to 1997, Connecticut also had a National Hockey League team, the Hartford Whalers, which became the Carolina Hurricanes. An American Hockey League (AHL) team, the Hartford Wolf Pack, was formed in 1997 and won the 1999–2000 AHL championship. The Connecticut Sun is a Women's National Basketball Association team. They are owned by the Native American tribe that runs the Mohegan Sun casino. The team plays its home games at the Mohegan Sun arena in Uncasville.

People who came to Connecticut from other countries have boosted the sport of soccer throughout the state. People from the West Indies have formed cricket teams.

In 1995 Connecticut hosted the Special Olympic Games in New Haven. The largest Special Olympics ever, they drew 7,000 athletes, 2,000 coaches, 45,000 volunteers, and more than 500,000 spectators. A number of the Olympians were natives of Connecticut. They included Kathy Ledwidge of Mystic, who has won medals in basketball, soccer, and volleyball, and Kim Musitano of Darien, who has won medals in tennis, bowling, and cross-country skiing.

Taking in a Connecticut Sun game is great indoor fun.

Whether at school, in the workplace, or on the athletic field, today's "Connecticut Yankees" find ways to share their talents and traditions while coming to know the state's heritage and to take part in its future.

Chapter Four

Government in the State of Steady Habits

Early on, people in Connecticut showed themselves to be independent thinkers who valued democratic principles. The Fundamental Orders declared that political authority came from "the free consent of the people." Later, the unique charter of 1662 set up a form of government that protected people from oppressive leaders.

Since Connecticut became a state, voters have continued to show their political independence. In 1989 journalist and political writer Harrison E. Salisbury commented, "The best thing about Connecticut people is that they ignore patterns. They are individualists, which makes it hard for politicians."

INSIDE GOVERNMENT

State government in Connecticut has three major branches: executive, legislative, and judicial.

The state capitol building in Hartford houses the State Senate Chambers, the Hall of the State House of Representatives, and the governor's offices.

Executive

The governor is the chief executive of the state. He or she is elected to a four-year term by a majority of voters in a general election. Governors initiate legislation, prepare an annual budget for the General Assembly, and appoint people to various positions. The governor lives in a nineteen-room mansion in Hartford, the state capital.

Connecticut, nicknamed the State of Steady Habits in colonial days, has tended to stick with its favorite leaders. Until recent years, there was no limit on the number of terms a governor could serve, and some served ten years or more. For instance, John Winthrop Jr., founder of New London, was governor of the colony in 1657 and again from 1659 to 1676. Later, Jonathan Trumbull served from 1769 to 1784. Trumbull was the only colonial governor to remain in office throughout the Revolutionary War and the second one chosen by the people rather than by an English king.

Trumbull and his wife Faith had two sons. Jonathan Trumbull II was a U.S. senator and governor of Connecticut, and his brother, John, became an artist after serving as a soldier in the Revolution. John's celebrated historical paintings include *Battle of Bunker's Hill* and *Capture of the Hessians at Trenton*. George Washington sat for him several times.

As of 2005 Connecticut is one of five states that have had two female governors. Governor Ella Grasso, a Democrat, was elected in 1974. Lieutenant Governor M. Jodi Rell, a Republican, stepped in after Governor John Rowland resigned in 2004. Rowland, who was serving his

Born in Watertown, Jonathan Trumbull served as Connecticut's governor from 1769 to 1784.

third term as governor, was threatened with impeachment after an investigation revealed that he had accepted gifts and money from state contractors. Under the law, Rell served out the rest of Rowland's term, which ended in 2006. She then ran for the office of governor that November and won.

Legislative

The law-making branch of Connecticut's state government has two houses, the Senate and the House of Representatives. As of 2005 there were 36 members of the Senate and 151 in the House, all elected by popular vote to two-year terms. A constitutional amendment passed in 1970 states that legislators must meet at least once a year. Either house may be called to meet in special sessions by the governor or by a majority of lawmakers in each chamber.

Upon being sworn into office, Governor Jodi Rell stated she will "work tirelessly with honor, dignity, and civility."

State budgets depend on revenues generated by the state income tax and high (6 percent) business and sales taxes. Towns collect property taxes for local budgets. Before 1991 Connecticut, unlike most other states, did not have a state income tax. When Governor Lowell Weicker introduced the tax, many citizens bitterly opposed it.

Weicker, a former Republican who had served as a U.S. senator, won election to the statehouse in 1990 as an Independent. Facing a major shortage in the state budget, Weicker asked the state legislature to pass the tax. *Time* magazine called Weicker the "Gutsiest Governor in America." He also was honored with the 1992 Profile in Courage Award, given each year by the President John F. Kennedy Library.

A WOMAN IN THE STATEHOUSE: ELLA GRASSO

Connecticut politics have provided some firsts through the years. In 1974 Ella Tambussi Grasso became the first woman to be elected governor of a state without being preceded in office by her husband. She was also the first Connecticut governor of Italian descent.

Born in Windsor Locks in 1919, Grasso was the daughter of immigrants. Her father, Giacomo, was a baker. She was an excellent student and received a scholarship to attend Mount Holyoke College in Massachusetts. After marrying Thomas Grasso in 1942, she gave birth to a son and a daughter.

Grasso began her public service career at age thirty-three when she was elected state representative. She then served for twelve years as secretary of the state and for four years in the U.S. Congress before running her winning campaign for governor in 1974.

During that same election, voters approved an amendment to the state's 1965 constitution making it illegal to discriminate on the basis of gender in Connecticut. The women's movement had worked to end discrimination in many areas of American life. Of that movement, Grasso said, "It's done a great deal in a short time to provide equal opportunity for women, and I feel I've been a beneficiary."

On December 31, 1980, Governor Grasso resigned for health reasons. She died of cancer the following year.

Judicial

Connecticut's constitution describes the functions of various state courts and gives the legislature the power to create lower courts. The Connecticut Supreme Court has a chief justice and six full-time associate justices. They hear cases brought by people who believe that their constitutional rights have been violated. The Appellate Court may hear cases on appeal (when the lower courts do not agree with the verdict, or decision) from lower courts.

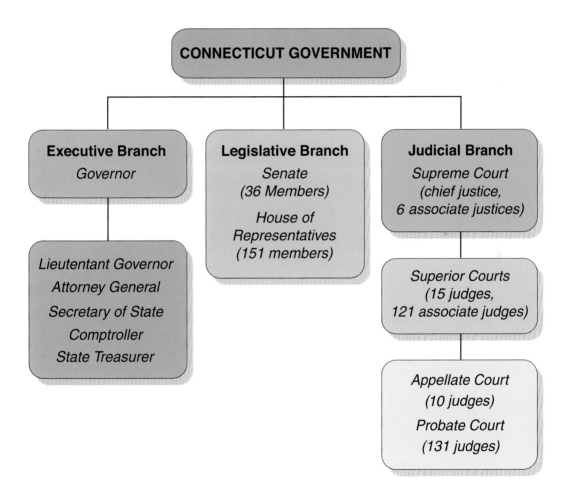

The major trial court for both adult and juvenile cases is a superior court, which has 121 full-time judges. These judges are first nominated by the governor, then appointed by the General Assembly. They serve eight-year terms. The superior court resolves civil (noncriminal) cases between individuals, as well as the criminal cases that the state brings against individuals.

The state has been governed by a constitution since 1639, first by the Fundamental Orders and then by the Charter of 1662. New constitutions were written in 1818 and in 1965. The latter has been amended regularly. One amendment, for example, lowered the voting age to eighteen. Another banned discrimination on the basis of sex and mental or physical disability, as well as race, religion, and national origin.

LOCAL GOVERNMENT

A form of government based on town meetings arose throughout colonial New England. In the 1600s and 1700s Connecticut residents were expected to attend town meetings several times a year. A drummer moved about to announce them. At these meetings, people discussed local matters such as fire protection—a serious concern in those days—and fencing to keep animals out of other people's fields. During these years, only men could vote. To qualify, a man had to own a certain amount of property or pay a certain amount of taxes.

Today, under the town government system, people elect their main officials, called selectmen (who can be men or women). Meetings, usually open to the public, can spark lively debates about zoning issues, parking problems, or whether to build a new school or playground.

Larger cities, including Bridgeport, Hartford, New Haven, and Stamford, elect mayors and city councils to run their governments.

CONNECTICUT BY COUNTY

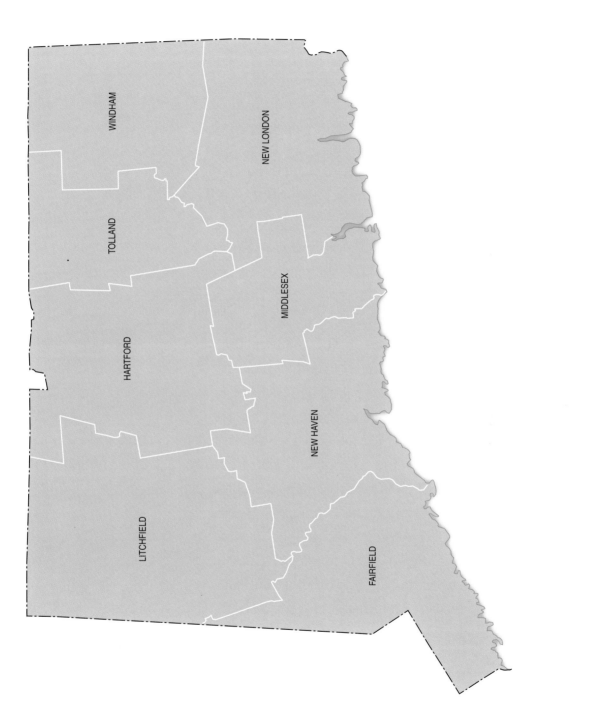

WINDHAM

NEW LONDON

TOLLAND

MIDDLESEX

HARTFORD

NEW HAVEN

LITCHFIELD

FAIRFIELD

In 1981 Thurman Milner was elected mayor of Hartford, thereby becoming the first African-American mayor of a New England city. Milner's great-great-great-great grandfather served in the Revolutionary War.

The referendum process allows citizens to take a more active role in politics. An election can be held after a certain number of registered voters signs a petition. For instance, in 2004, citizens in Wethersfield voted on a referendum to appropriate money to renovate their town hall, library, and community center. The results were 1,477 "yes" votes and 129 "no" votes. In recent years, voters in several towns also have used this process to try to lower their property taxes.

NATIONAL POLITICS

Connecticut shows its independent mind at election time, with many citizens voting across party lines, claiming that they "vote the person, not the party." From 1850 to the early 1930s Republicans usually received more votes in both state and national elections. That changed during the Great Depression, when voters elected Democrats to lead their state and to represent them in Washington, D.C. After the 1930s, Connecticut's electoral votes went to both Democrats and Republicans. Then, in the presidential elections of 1992, 1996, 2000, and 2004, the state voted for the Democratic ticket, despite the fact that citizens elected a Republican governor during those years.

The League of Women Voters encourages voter registration at a street fair in Wallingford.

Since 1987 an increasing number of voters are calling themselves unaffiliated—not a member of any party. Connecticut is one of seven states with a plurality of such voters. And though the state once favored Republican candidates in state elections, it had a Democratic majority in the statehouse during the early 2000s. Connecticut has sent more Democrats than Republicans to serve in the U.S. Congress. As of 2005 two Democrats, Christopher Dodd and Joseph Lieberman, had been serving in the U.S. Senate since 1981 and 1988, respectively.

MEETING SOCIAL NEEDS

One of the greatest challenges for lawmakers and citizens is dealing with social problems that trouble certain parts of the state. Poverty plagues some rural areas and small cities as well as large cities like Bridgeport and Hartford.

These problems have affected minorities more severely than whites. During the 1950s and 1960s the civil rights movement swept across the United States. People worked to end racism and discriminatory practices in jobs, housing, and schools throughout Connecticut.

In 1957 a group of black ministers joined forces with the National Association for the Advancement of Colored People to elect more African Americans to public office in Connecticut. African Americans became more numerous in politics and law enforcement, on welfare boards, and in school administration.

Inequities in the education system also have received more attention. Since the early 1900s public schools in Connecticut have been under local control, and young people have been assigned to schools in their communities. These local school systems raise taxes to fund education, while the state sends additional money to schools on the basis of need.

The state's poorer citizens tend to live in its cities, so urban schools have a disproportionate number of minority and lower-income students. These areas have poorer tax bases, resulting in less money for schools. The unequal funding has meant that students in wealthy suburban schools have more modern textbooks and equipment, more choices of courses and activities, and better-maintained facilities than students in poor urban schools. They can also offer higher salaries to teachers and administrators.

The state wants to resolve district funding problems so that all Connecticut students receive a quality education.

Like many states, Connecticut is seeking solutions. Should the state make sure that all schools receive equal funding? What about school choice, a system in which students receive vouchers they can use to attend any school in their state or region? Should students be transported from local schools to regional schools in order to create more diverse mixtures of whites and minorities?

In 1996 the state supreme court heard an important education case called *Sheff v. O'Neill*. The case originated in 1989 when a group in Hartford, including an African-American student named Milo Sheff, filed a lawsuit against the state. Sheff's attorneys claimed that racial segregation in Connecticut's schools denied all children a quality education.

The court ruled in Sheff's favor and directed the state legislature to find remedies for the situation. Since the court's ruling, a program called Project Choice has let some students voluntarily attend schools outside their districts. Students compete for a limited number of spots in schools regarded as "desirable." More magnet schools opened throughout the state, and they had waiting lists of both urban and suburban students from surrounding districts. Magnet schools offer special programs, such as Asian studies, environmental science, or the arts, to attract a diverse group of students. In addition, schools in neighboring districts have sponsored joint field trips and other activities so that students can meet peers from different backgrounds.

Critics complain that these programs have not solved the problem of racial and ethnic isolation in public schools, nor have they adequately improved urban schools. Some critics propose more state funding to ensure high-quality schools in low-income areas. In 2003 the state legislature agreed to make funds available to expand both the magnet schools and Project Choice. Finding ways to offer all children a quality education remains a challenge.

Chapter Five

A Changing Economy

From an economy based on agriculture and trade, Connecticut evolved to become an industrial state known for its electronics, metalworking, plastics, and transportation equipment. With relatively few natural resources, the state relied on manufacturing and other kinds of jobs and businesses, such as the insurance industry. During the twentieth century the state's economy changed further to include more service and technology businesses, and manufacturing, agriculture, and fishing played lesser roles. Tourism contributes about $4 billion a year to the state's economy.

FROM FARMS TO FACTORIES

Early settlers worked their own farms to provide food for their families. They exchanged surplus produce, meat, and milk for other things they needed. As the population grew, people in settled areas could not obtain enough farmland to support the typical large family. To preserve their independent way of life, people moved to unsettled parts of the state where land was still available. Others planted crops with a higher yield per acre, or they joined with neighbors to share equipment and trade the different crops they produced.

Stamford attracts many financial companies. This is the trading floor of Union Bank of Switzerland.

During Connecticut's early days, settlers built their own farms and ate food grown near their homes.

By the mid-1700s people in both rural areas and towns were running businesses to serve the growing population. Storekeepers offered household goods, as well as imported sugar, molasses, tea, and spices. Taverns and inns served travelers. Some enterprising families became wealthy in shipbuilding or fishing businesses or through trade.

2003 GROSS STATE PRODUCT: $174 Million

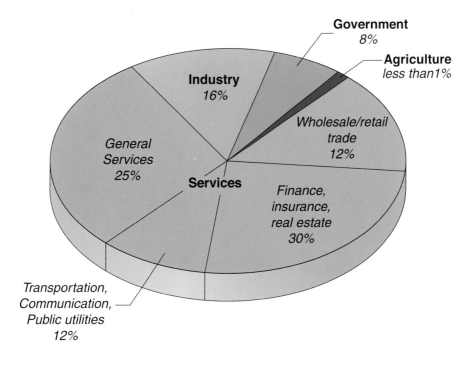

Government 8%

Agriculture less than 1%

Industry 16%

Wholesale/retail trade 12%

General Services 25%

Services

Finance, insurance, real estate 30%

Transportation, Communication, Public utilities 12%

The economy became more industrialized during the eighteenth and nineteenth centuries. Immigrants from Europe came to help build canals and railroads or took jobs in stone quarries and factories. Some started businesses, working as peddlers, tailors, carpenters, grocers, bakers, or farmers. Skilled weavers and loom-fixers worked in the silk mills. In 1806 the first planned factory town in the United States, called Humphreyville, was created in Seymour.

Silk was produced in Connecticut for more than two hundred years. These textile workers sort and clean fibers from silk cocoons in South Manchester.

Large manufacturing centers sprang up in Bridgeport, Danbury, Waterbury, Stamford, Norwalk, Hartford, New Haven, New Britain, Manchester, and Middletown. They produced ammunition, pistols, revolvers, rifles, clocks, watches, hardware, tools, machine tools, heavy industrial machinery, and other products.

Creative ideas and inventions spurred the growing economy. The U.S. government first began issuing patents in 1790, and between that year and 1930, Connecticut led the nation in the number of patents issued per capita. Among the many firsts in the state were the cast-iron stove foundry set up in Stamford (1830), the first portable typewriter (1843), and the first machine-made horseshoe nails, produced in Hartford in 1866.

Diverse businesses created jobs and built up the state's economy. The Fuller Brush Company, now a global business, had its roots in Hartford, where Alfred C. Fuller set up his brush-making factory in 1906. The Pepperidge Farm Company was founded in 1937 when Margaret Rudkin started baking bread to sell in her Fairfield kitchen. By 1947 the company was operating a large modern bakery in Norwalk, where it still has its headquarters. With over $1 billion in sales annually, this multinational food-products business sells baked goods, snack foods, and frozen breads and desserts.

Many other international companies maintain corporate offices in Connecticut. Some of the best-known are General Electric, International Paper, Pitney Bowes, Conair, and Xerox.

As of 2003 more than 150,000 people work in Connecticut's manufacturing industry producing a wide variety of goods, ranging from toy trains to silverware to chemicals to optical instruments.

An early advertisement for Fuller Brushes, a Hartford-based company that still produces "the best products of their kind in the world."

Called the Provisions State during the Revolutionary War, Connecticut has continued to supply the nation's armed forces. Through the years, tens of thousands of people have held jobs that depended on federal military and defense-related spending.

Jet aircraft engines and helicopters made in Connecticut are used for civilian transportation as well as military purposes. For example, Pratt & Whitney is a leading manufacturer of engines for commercial and military aircraft, including F-15 fighter jets. In 1860 two machinists founded the company, which is headquartered in East Hartford. Now a division of United Technologies, Pratt & Whitney produced more than 500,000 piston and jet engines between 1925 and 2005.

Connecticut became the world's submarine capital after the first modern submarine was built in Groton. In 1900 financier Isaac Rice founded his Electric Boat Company there to develop the fifty-four-foot submersible vessel John Philip Holland had invented. Later, the company merged with the New London Ship & Engine Company to make diesel engines and other parts for submarines and commercial ships. During and shortly after World War I, the company filled orders for eighty-five submarines from the U.S. Navy. In 1934 workers at Electric Boat made the first welded submarine, which was delivered to the U.S. Navy. During World War II the company made seventy-four submarines and 398 PT boats for the military. Between 1951 and 2005 Electric Boat introduced more sophisticated classes of submarines, including the *Nautilus*, which was the world's first atomic-powered submarine, followed by the *Polaris* and the *Trident*. A large portion of the U.S. Navy's *Seawolf* submarine contract, which was worth $2.4 billion, came into Connecticut.

The Naval Submarine Base New London's construction yard is the site for the building of nuclear submarines.

In addition to naval vessels, Connecticut produces world-famous aircraft. Between 1938 and 1945 male and female workers in the state produced 12,500 Corsair F-4U fighter planes. Ninety percent of the components used in these planes were made in Connecticut. In 2005 state legislators passed a bill making the Corsair F-4U the official state airplane. Former pilot Nick Maniero flew fifty-one missions in the South Pacific during World War II. In 2005 he recalled flying two hundred miles over the ocean back to his base after enemy fire blew the tail off his Corsair: "At 21,000 feet, it could fly 425 miles per hour and it was stable. You could trim it up and fly it with no hands."

The Corsair was one of the newest U.S. Navy fighter planes during World War II. Its engine was manufactured by Vought-Sikorsky in Connecticut.

Companies founded by Russian American Igor Sikorsky also provided aircraft for military and civilian use. Sikorsky brought his business to Stratford in 1929; in 1939 it was reorganized as Vought-Sikorsky. This company produced fighter aircraft, including the V-173 and the F4U-ID Corsair, used extensively during World War II. The company's VS-300 helicopter, considered the forerunner of modern helicopters, made its first flight in 1940. In 1943 the company split, and Vought focused on military aircraft while Sikorsky Aircraft Corporation designed and built the helicopters for which it became famous. Igor Sikorsky refined the technology and design of these aircraft to make them more practical. By the end of World War II, the U.S. Army had ordered four hundred of the company's R-4 helicopters.

Sikorsky helicopters also were flown during the Korean and Vietnam wars. For forty-seven years, the company provided the Marine One helicopters that transport U.S. presidents and their families. Igor Sikorsky Memorial Airport in Stratford is named for this aircraft pioneer.

EARNING A LIVING

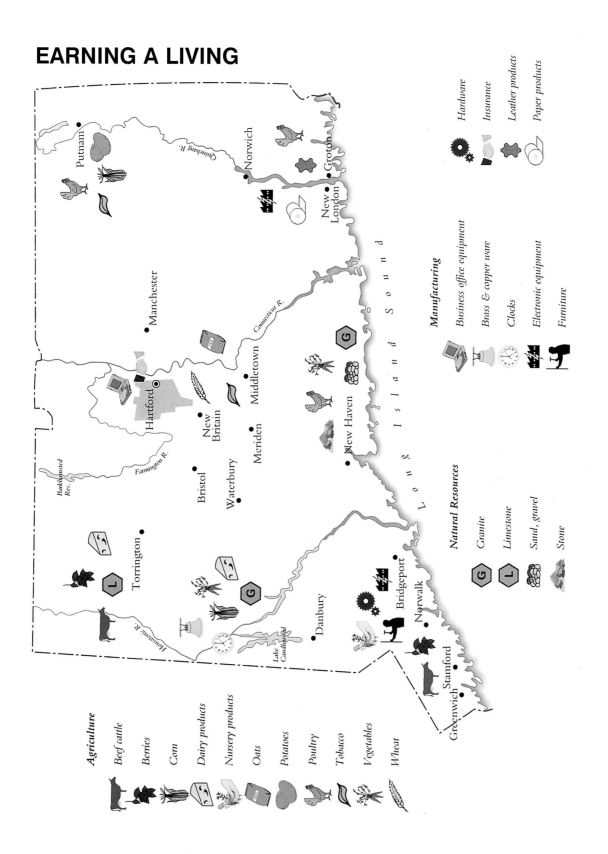

Hardware
Insurance
Leather products
Paper products

Manufacturing
Business office equipment
Brass & copper ware
Clocks
Electronic equipment
Furniture

Natural Resources
Granite
Limestone
Sand, gravel
Stone

Agriculture
Beef cattle
Berries
Corn
Dairy products
Nursery products
Oats
Potatoes
Poultry
Tobacco
Vegetables
Wheat

Putnam
Norwich
Groton
New London
Manchester
Middletown
Hartford
New Britain
Meriden
New Haven
Bristol
Waterbury
Torrington
Danbury
Bridgeport
Norwalk
Stamford
Greenwich

Quinebaug R.
Connecticut R.
Farmington R.
Housatonic R.
Barkhamsted Res.
Lake Candlewood
Long Island Sound

FINANCIAL INDUSTRIES

Significant revenues come from the real estate, banking, and financial industries. Hartford has been an important center of America's insurance industry since the late 1700s, when sea captains decided to pool sums of money to offset their losses if a ship was wrecked or lost. These ships sailed to and from the Caribbean out of Connecticut's river and sea ports.

Fire insurance followed coverage for marine losses. The first official insurance firm, the Hartford Fire Insurance Company, was organized in 1794. Later, companies offered still more types of insurance: life, accident, health, and casualty. By the 1990s thousands of employees worked at about thirty-six Hartford-based firms. As of 2005, 106 insurance companies were based in the state.

AGRICULTURE

Farms have been on the decline in Connecticut. Since 1800 the amount of land devoted to farming has decreased from about 80 percent to 12 percent. As of 2004 there were 4,200 farms in Connecticut, and agriculture contributed about $2.2 billion per year to the economy. Connecticut's farm products include eggs and dairy products, chickens, beef cattle, vegetables, fruits, hay, and tobacco.

As of 2003 about 51 percent of the 360,000 farm acres in the state was being used for dairy or dairy support, and there were 174 dairy farms. The second largest use of farmland—about 12 percent—was devoted to growing flowers, shrubs, and other products for the greenhouse and nursery markets. Several vineyards operate in Connecticut to produce grapes for wine.

The most valuable crop per acre is tobacco. Many Puerto Ricans who came to Connecticut for seasonal work, or to settle permanently, worked in this industry. Tobacco growers, including the Topper Cigar Company in

Many of Connecticut's flowers and plants are grown in nurseries throughout the state.

Meriden, benefited from rapidly rising cigar sales that began during the mid-1990s. The Toppers' family business opened in 1896 and is one of the longest-running family-owned cigar businesses in the United States. President Chris Topper said, "There were lean times when many factories got out of the business. But the consistency of our product enabled us to survive and expand."

FISHING AND AQUACULTURE

Commercial fishing remains part of the Connecticut economy. Fishermen catch about 3,600 tons of seafood annually. They harvest hard-shell clams and oysters, as well as flounder, cod, and lobster.

Harbor and stream pollution and diseases have affected seafood businesses, including about 41,000 acres of oyster beds off the coast of Long Island Sound. In 1997 two fatal parasitic infections killed nearly 90 percent of the oyster population. Only 32,000 bushels were harvested. Some oyster fishermen turned to clams to make up for the loss.

Fishers empty their catch of oysters from the Long Island Sound.

After 1997 some businesses built new kinds of offshore hatcheries and began raising disease-resistant strains of oysters. Companies also began raising oysters in cages that are submerged in the waters of the sound. As of 2005 oyster production brought in about $62 million a year. Connecticut's oyster crop ranked first in the nation in dollar value and second only to Louisiana in quantity.

The multi-million dollar lobster business also has suffered. In 1998 fishers saw rising numbers of dead and dying lobsters in the sound. The problem worsened the next year, when so many lobsters died that fishers and dealers were put out of business. Reproduction rates also declined. Scientists concluded that a parasite, along with other environmental factors, probably caused this lobster die-off. Although fishing conditions improved somewhat after 1999, they remained poor. In 2000 the Long Island Sound Lobster Research Initiative was funded to study the problem. They want to know how disease, water temperatures, pesticides, and inadequate oxygen affect the shellfish.

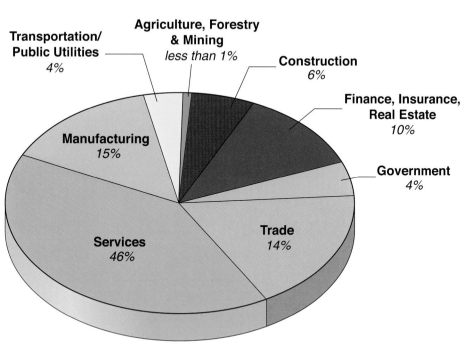

CONNECTICUT WORKFORCE

Transportation/ Public Utilities 4%

Agriculture, Forestry & Mining less than 1%

Construction 6%

Finance, Insurance, Real Estate 10%

Government 4%

Manufacturing 15%

Trade 14%

Services 46%

ECONOMIC CHALLENGES

Besides the Great Depression of the 1930s, Connecticut has been hit with economic recessions through the years. During the 1950s and 1960s, jobs left the state when textile companies and others moved south or abroad to save money on labor and other costs. Some people left Connecticut to work elsewhere. About 116,000 manufacturing jobs were lost between 1989 and 1999.

Other jobs were lost during the early 1990s after the federal government cut defense spending. For more than forty years, the United States and the communist-governed Soviet Union were engaged in the cold war. Both sides maintained strong military forces and weapons, including nuclear warheads, offensive and defensive missiles, and submarines. The Reagan administration

(1981–1989) increased military spending. Connecticut industries received billions of dollars in government contracts. The fall of communism in Eastern Europe brought an end to the cold war and the trimming of America's defense arsenal. In less than ten years, Connecticut was receiving about one-third of the money for defense spending that it once had received from the federal government.

In May 2005 the Norwich Bulletin *ran a special edition that focused on the closing of the submarine naval base in Groton.*

In Groton, General Dynamics Electric Boat Division laid off thousands of workers. It lost large defense contracts, which once had provided about half the jobs in that region. By the late 1990s, new contracts had brought back some of these jobs. In May 2005 the Pentagon recommended that the submarine base at Groton be closed. State legislators worked to ensure that Connecticut kept its submarine base. That August, a government panel studying the issue voted to keep the naval submarine base open.

The changes that occur with a global economy also have affected jobs in Connecticut. As large corporations bought smaller companies, they often downsized and laid off workers and even shut down these companies. This was the fate of some Naugatuck River valley brass companies that had operated for more than a century. In other cases, corporations moved their manufacturing operations to Mexico or other countries and replaced full-time workers with part-time workers. Some insurance companies in Connecticut have laid off employees and replaced them with people in India and other lower-wage countries who can work via satellite hookup.

As a result, the state lost more than 200,000 jobs—about 10 percent of its total jobs—between 1989 and 1995. Job loss hurt local economies because people paid lower taxes, leading to budget cuts in the community and less money for services. People with less money to spend also cannot buy goods and services that keep other businesses going.

Downturns in the economy hit poorer communities especially hard. In late 2005 the unemployment rate was around 5.1 percent, compared to the national rate of 5.0 percent, but unemployment was higher in Hartford, New Haven, Waterbury, and certain other cities. Since the 1980s the incomes of poor and lower middle-class families in Connecticut have fallen, while people in the top income brackets have seen increases.

Noting the slight decrease in the unemployment rate early in 2005, Governor M. Jodi Rell called the statistics "encouraging." She noted, however, that "newspapers continue to carry news about possible cuts and relocations, and we are working every day to retain and increase the number of meaningful good-paying jobs in our state."

The face of Connecticut's labor force has changed a great deal since the mid-twentieth century. In 1950, 3 percent of all jobs were in agriculture, with 49 percent in manufacturing and 48 percent in services. By 2000 only 1 percent of all jobs were in agriculture, and manufacturing accounted for 15 percent. The greatest share—46 percent—were in service businesses.

As times change, the state looks for new goods and services that will bring a healthy economy and sustain the 3.5 million people who call Connecticut home. The state looks toward its strengths, which include a well-educated labor force and the nation's highest percentage of employment in technology-based industries. Geographically, the state also benefits from its excellent business location, as well as the innovative thinkers, skilled business managers, and workers in various industries and fields of endeavor.

Chapter Six

Places to Visit

Connecticut's compact size makes it possible to cross the state in just two or three hours, moving from quiet, traditional villages to bustling cities, from a ski resort to a seaport, all in the same day. It has been said that a motorist driving on the highway is never more than thirty minutes away from a state park.

Residents of the Nutmeg State are connected by a broad highway system, including the Connecticut Turnpike and the Merritt Parkway. The curving, tree-lined Merritt is considered one of the most scenic highways in the United States. In the northeast, Connecticut State Route 169 is on the list of America's Scenic Byways. Those who prefer trains can commute on more than 610 miles of railroad track, including the Metro-North Railroad, which runs between Grand Central Terminal in New York City and New Haven, with stops in between.

The train is also a convenient way to get to plays, concerts, and sporting events. Young performers who live in southern Connecticut may take the train when they perform in a Broadway play or film commercials, many of which are made in New York.

Historic Sheffield Island Lighthouse can be visited by taking a short ferry ride from Norwalk.

In recent decades many Connecticut residents have discovered that they can go "on vacation" in their own state. They are able to enjoy day and weekend trips near home.

FAIRFIELD COUNTY AND THE GOLD COAST

At the southwest corner of the state, along Long Island Sound and close to New York City, lies Fairfield County, including the "Gold Coast." This row of wealthy communities includes Greenwich, Darien, New Canaan, Wilton, Westport, and Fairfield. Mostly residential, these communities boast fine shopping areas and popular restaurants featuring various kinds of cuisine. During summer or fall, visitors driving along country roads in Fairfield County will find outdoor flea markets, antique stores, and farm stands selling fruits and vegetables.

In Norwalk a nineteenth-century factory was restored and turned into the Maritime Aquarium. This aquarium holds live exhibits of seals and other sea creatures, large and small, that can be found in Long Island Sound and on the Connecticut shore. Boats and other exhibits show visitors more about maritime life and history.

The city of Bridgeport contains several museums and landmarks. Downtown, the Discovery Museum features hands-on science exhibits and rooms where visitors can find out about nuclear energy, electricity, and magnetism. Beardsley Zoological Gardens features typical farm animals, along with wild and rare species. There is a re-creation of a tropical rain forest, as well as woodlands, a large lake, and a garden.

Visitors to the Barnum Museum can trace the career of the great showman Phineas Taylor (P. T.) Barnum, who was born in Bethel, Connecticut, in 1810. Exhibits explain the history of circuses and feature pictures of people and businesses in Bridgeport from earlier days.

A visit to the Maritime Aquarium in Norwalk will bring you face to face with seals, sharks, and over one thousand other marine animals.

Well-designed nature centers can be found throughout Connecticut. The Audubon Center in Greenwich, for example, covers 280 acres of woodlands, with rare tree specimens, meadows, ponds, and streams. Visitors to the center especially like the working beehive and bird observation windows. In 2003 this facility opened its new $8 million Kimberlin Nature Education Center, which includes interactive nature exhibits and sponsors lectures, workshops, and summer camps.

NEW HAVEN COUNTY

Moving east, along the southern coast of the state, you reach New Haven County. This area is rich in history and has become a center for the arts.

The Yale University Art Gallery, which opened in 1832, was the first university art museum in the Western Hemisphere. Starting with one hundred paintings, a gift from artist John Trumbull, the museum built a collection of early American and modern art. The Yale Center for British Art and British Studies has amassed the largest collection of British art outside the British Isles. Also at Yale is the Peabody Museum of Natural History, known for its Native American displays and Great Hall of Dinosaurs.

On the coast south of New Haven is Branford, which was founded in 1644. Vacationers have long enjoyed visiting Stony Creek, a typical New England fishing village in the town. Boat tour guides tell old tales about the pirates who raided ships along the coast centuries ago. The Thimble Islands of Branford are said to hold lost pirate treasure. Even if you don't find buried treasure, you can fish or sit and watch the gulls, cormorants, and herons find their dinner.

MIDDLESEX COUNTY

To the east of Branford and up the Connecticut River lies Hadlyme, the site of a simulated medieval castle that draws some hundred thousand visitors each year. Gillette's Castle was the home of William Gillette, a stage actor and playwright of the early 1900s. The fieldstone castle, built between 1914 and 1919, rises from a bluff over a bank of the Connecticut River. The outside is adorned with fairy-castle turrets, arches, and fountains. Its twenty-four rooms contain fancy carvings, fine woodwork, and elegant furniture. Gillette, famous for portraying fictional detective Sherlock Holmes, decorated a room in his castle to look like Holmes's London study.

Another notable building in nearby East Haddam is the Goodspeed Opera House, a Victorian replica of a famous opera house in Paris.

Gillette Castle is a twenty-four room mansion built with local fieldstone. Visitors can tour the castle as well as its grounds.

The building was restored as a museum, then turned into a theater. Shows were brought there by steamer from New York City during the early 1900s.

A visit to East Haddam is not complete without seeing the famous bell at Saint Stephen's Episcopal Church. It was made 815 CE and originally hung in a Spanish monastery. The bell was taken to New York City on a nineteenth-century trading ship, and William Pratt, a ship chandler, shipped it to his hometown of East Haddam. It is thought to be the world's oldest church bell.

THE SUBMARINE CAPITAL

On the coast near the eastern border of Connecticut is the town of Groton, where visitors can learn more about American maritime history. Located here are the U.S. naval submarine base, the naval submarine school, and the USS *Nautilus* memorial. The amazing and powerful nuclear-powered *Nautilus* was used both as a defense weapon and for underwater exploration thousands of feet beneath the Arctic ice. Also on display are submarines from the days of the Revolutionary War to the present.

Visitors can actually test seawater and learn how to identify various sea creatures when they climb aboard Project Oceanology, located at Groton's University of Connecticut campus at Avery Point. Camps for young people and educational cruises are offered throughout the summer, while seal-watch cruises take place during winter months.

At nearby Fort Griswold Battlefield State Park is a monument to soldiers killed during a 1781 massacre by British troops. A museum details the history of that event and also features the history of the whaling industry.

The USS Nautilus *can be visited at the Submarine Force Museum in Groton.*

PLACES TO SEE

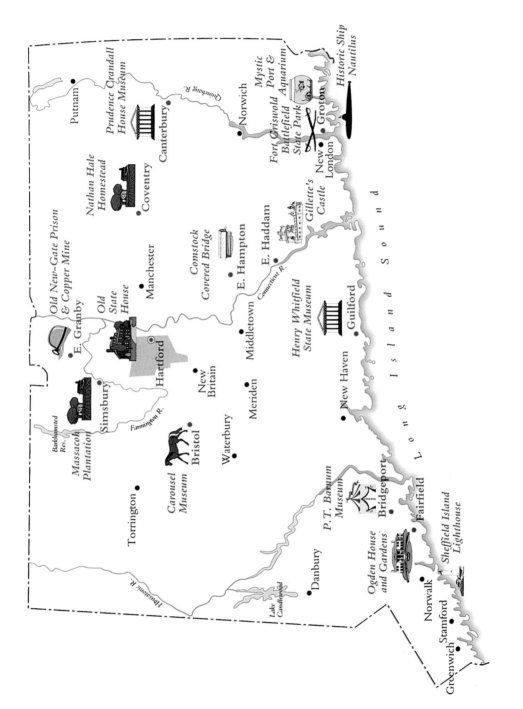

Putnam

Prudence Crandall House Museum

Canterbury

Quinebaug R.

Norwich

Mystic Port & Aquarium

Historic Ship Nautilus

Nathan Hale Homestead

Coventry

Fort Griswold Battlefield State Park

Groton

New London

Old New-Gate Prison & Copper Mine

Comstock Covered Bridge

E. Hampton

E. Haddam

Gillette's Castle

Manchester

Connecticut R.

Long Island Sound

E. Granby

Old State House

Hartford

Henry Whitfield State Museum

Guilford

Simsbury

New Britain

Meriden

New Haven

Farmington R.

Barkhamsted Res.

Massacoh Plantation

Bristol

Waterbury

Carousel Museum

Torrington

P. T. Barnum Museum

Bridgeport

Fairfield

Sheffield Island Lighthouse

Danbury

Ogden House and Gardens

Norwalk

Housatonic R.

Lake Candlewood

Stamford

Greenwich

Because the earliest settlements were built in central Connecticut, many historical sites, monuments, old buildings, and museums are found here. Hartford, the state's oldest city and its capital, holds much of interest, both old and new. The oldest free art museum in the country, Wadsworth Atheneum, was built here in 1842. The Connecticut Historical Society Museum is also located in the state capital. Many visitors come to see the former homes of the well-known authors Mark Twain and Harriet Beecher Stowe.

The elegant old statehouse was designed by America's first native-born architect, Charles Bulfinch. Built in 1796, it is the oldest statehouse in the United States and is listed as a national landmark. This building was erected on the same site where the Fundamental Orders of 1638–1639 were ratified and served as the capitol from 1796 to 1878. Here General George Washington planned important strategy for the Revolutionary War and his campaign in Yorktown. Connecticut delegates met at the statehouse to discuss ratifying the United States Constitution.

Under the direction of Wilson (Bill) Faude, the old statehouse was renovated between 1992 and 1996. A carillon on the roof now plays music and lets off a booming noise when an important news event takes place. Like modern Connecticut itself, the building celebrates diversity and blends old with new, with its historical exhibits, Latino artwork, and elegant Great Senate Room. The building is used by people in the community for debates, speeches, weddings, and school functions. Says Faude, "This building is to serve people. This is not a museum for . . . pewter spoons."

The present capitol opened in 1878, and the General Assembly first met there the next year. This newer building is fashioned of Connecticut marble, with statues and medallions on the outside showing important

Bushnell Memorial Park in Hartford is the setting for the Connecticut State Capitol building, designed by architect Richard M. Upjohn.

TEN LARGEST CITIES

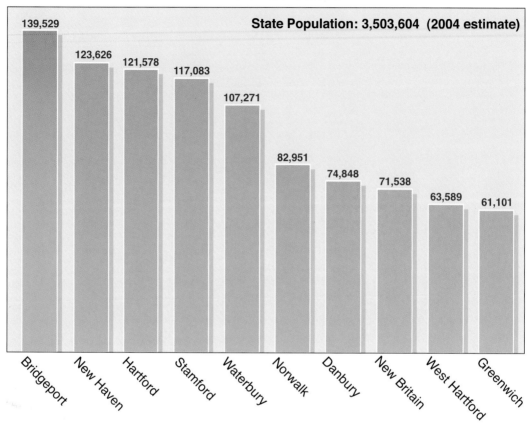

State Population: 3,503,604 (2004 estimate)

- Bridgeport: 139,529
- New Haven: 123,626
- Hartford: 121,578
- Stamford: 117,083
- Waterbury: 107,271
- Norwalk: 82,951
- Danbury: 74,848
- New Britain: 71,538
- West Hartford: 63,589
- Greenwich: 61,101

people and events in the state's history. Objects of interest inside are the camp bed that French general Lafayette used during the Revolutionary War and a figurehead from the ship *Hartford*, which was commanded by Admiral David Farragut, a leading naval commander for the Union Army during the Civil War.

Summer visitors who love flowers will relish the stunning Elizabeth Park Rose Gardens. This park, with 15,000 rose bushes and more than 800 varieties, was the first municipal rose garden in the United States. Other areas of the park hold rock gardens and beds of flowers, plants, and herbs.

Southeast of Hartford, Bristol contains the fascinating New England Carousel Museum. A large display of carousel-related items shows the kinds of rides children enjoyed in amusement parks around 1900. Some of the horses and other figures are works of art, carefully carved and painted with precise details. A workshop shows visitors how carousel figures are made.

HILLS AND VILLAGE GREENS

The steep, picturesque hills and quaint villages of northern Connecticut attract many visitors, including artists. One charming feature remaining in many old towns is the village green, also called a common because these acres of open land in the center of town were owned in common by all the citizens. Outdoor community activities, including meetings, military drills, and public hangings, took place there. Some were used for grazing cows. Today they may hold concerts, exhibits, or art fairs.

The town of Cornwall boasts an old covered bridge that spans the Housatonic River. Many artists have drawn or painted the bridge or been inspired by the forested hills around Cornwall.

Another town in northern Connecticut, Simsbury, has become famous as a figure-skating and hockey center. Skaters from around the world, including world and Olympic champions, have lived in

At 242 feet long, the covered bridge in Cornwall has been in use since 1864.

Simsbury and trained at this rink. Ice shows at the International Skating Center of Connecticut attract visitors from around the country and the world.

Called the "Quiet Corner," northeastern Connecticut is known for its rolling hills, woodland trails, and historic sites. Visitors to Canterbury can see the Prudence Crandall Museum, which honors the courage of the woman who was named Connecticut's state heroine in 1995. In 1833 Crandall opened the first academy in New England for African-American girls. She and her students faced strong opposition from the community, including mob violence, and Crandall was arrested twice for refusing to close the school.

Tolland County is known for its charming historical towns and rustic natural beauty, with opportunities for outdoor activities year-round. In Coventry visitors can see the Nathan Hale Homestead, one of the nation's most stately colonial homes. Hale grew up here with his nine brothers and sisters before he left home to attend Yale University and then to serve in the Continental Army.

In nearby Bolton people enjoy the fine ice cream emporium located at the Fish Family Farm Creamery and Dairy. They can see how the staff at this working dairy farm milks, pasteurizes, and bottles milk and makes its own ice cream.

The main campus of the University of Connecticut at Storrs is known for its diverse collection of trees and themed gardens. Its little Stone House features stone specimens from every town in the state, as well as from all fifty states. At the Geology Park, visitors can see a set of dinosaur footprints found in Connecticut.

Of course there is much more to do in Connecticut. People can go hiking, boating, fishing, camping, or swimming in warm weather.

During wintertime they can ski in the mountains of the north. There are restored colonial and Native American villages, dozens of art and science museums, homes where famous people once lived and worked, and car, boat, and balloon races to watch. There are miles of winding rivers and state parks to explore. In the small but vigorous state called Connecticut, there are enough sources of fun and learning to fill several lifetimes.

Students canoe the Long Island Sound.

THE FLAG: The flag shows the state coat of arms on a field of azure. Below is a streamer that bears the state motto in blue letters: "He who transplanted still sustains." The state flag was adopted in 1897.

THE SEAL: The state seal is in the form of an ellipse. Around the outer border are the Latin words Sigillum Reipublicae Connecticutensis, *which mean "Seal of the Republic of Connecticut." In the center of the ellipse, three staked grapevines form a V. The grapevines symbolize the culture of the Old World (Europe) being transplanted to the New World. Below the grapevine is a streamer with the state motto. The seal was adopted in 1931.*

State Survey

Statehood: January 9, 1788

Origin of Name: *Connecticut* comes from a Native American word meaning "beside the long tidal river." The river referred to is the Connecticut River, which divides the state in half from north to south.

Nicknames: Constitution State, Nutmeg State, Land of Steady Habits

Capital: Hartford

Motto: He Who Transplanted Still Sustains

Bird: American robin

Animal: Sperm whale

Insect: Praying mantis

Flower: Mountain laurel

Tree: White oak

Mineral: Garnet

Ship: USS *Nautilus*

American robin

Mountain laurel

YANKEE DOODLE

During the Revolutionary War, British soldiers sang mocking verses to poke fun at the Americans. American soldier Edward Banks, on hearing one song, decided that he would write new lyrics that the Yankees could sing back at the British. It is this version of "Yankee Doodle" that has gone down in American history and became Connecticut's unofficial state song.

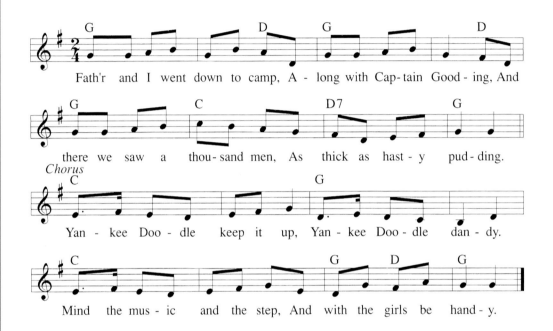

GEOGRAPHY

Highest Point: 2,380 feet above sea level, at Mount Frissell

Lowest Point: Sea level, at Long Island Sound in Salisbury

Area: 5,544 square miles

Greatest Distance North to South: 75 miles

Greatest Distance East to West: 90 miles

Bordering States: Massachusetts to the north, Rhode Island to the east, New York to the west

Hottest Recorded Temperature: 106°F at Danbury on July 15, 1995

Coldest Recorded Temperature: −32°F on February 16, 1943

Average Annual Precipitation: 44 to 48 inches

Major Rivers: Connecticut, Farmington, Housatonic, Naugatuck, Pequonnock, Pootatuck, Quinebaug, Salmon, Shetucket, Thames

Major Lakes: Candlewood, Gaillard, Lillinnoah, Mansfield Hollow, Zoar

Trees: Ash, aspen, beech, birch, cedar, dogwood, elm, hemlock, hickory, hop hornbeam, horse chestnut, ironwood, maple, oak, pine, sycamore, tulip, walnut, willow

Wild Plants: Barberry, raspberry, bloodroot, blueberry, cowslip, hepatica, huckleberry, Indian pipe, jack-in-the-pulpit, juniper berry, lady's slipper, lupine, mountain laurel, pennyroyal, sheep laurel, grape fern, trailing arbutus, wild raisin

Animals: Beaver, black bear, chipmunk, cottontail rabbit, coyote, fisher martin, fox, mink, muskrat, opossum, otter, raccoon, skunk, squirrel, white-tailed deer, woodchuck

Birds: Bald eagle, bluebird, bluejay, bobwhite, cardinal, chickadee, chimney swift, cooper's hawk, crow, duck, egret, goldfinch, heron, meadowlark, oriole, osprey, owl, partridge, quail, red-tailed hawk, ring-necked pheasant, robin, ruffed grouse, sparrow, thrush, warbler, whipporwill, wild turkey, woodcock, wood duck, woodpecker

Fish: Blackfish, bluefish, bluegill, brook trout, brown trout, bullhead, butterfish, calico bass, cod, flounder, largemouth bass, mackerel, perch, pickerel, pollack, porgy, rainbow trout, shad, smallmouth bass, smelt, sockeye salmon, striped bass, sunfish, swordfish

Reptiles: Atlantic green turtle, bog turtle, Eastern bog turtle, Eastern garter snake, Eastern hog nose snake, Eastern ribbon snake, five-lined skink, Northern brown snake, Northern copperhead, smooth green snake, timber rattlesnake, wood turtle,

Endangered Animals: Bald eagle, bog turtle, Indiana bat, least shrew, long-eared owl, peregrine falcon, red-headed woodpecker, sparrow

Skunk

Endangered Plants: Balsam fir, bog willow, Devil's bit, dwarf mistletoe, golden seal, hairy lip fern, Indian paintbrush, large-leaved sandwort, panic grass, red mulberry, rough-leaved aster, showy lady's-slipper, side-oats grama-grass, green milkweed

TIMELINE

Connecticut History

1614 Adriaen Block sails up Connecticut River and claims surrounding land for Holland.

1633 The Dutch build a fur-trading post at Hartford; the English build their first settlement at Windsor.

1637 John Mason and his army defeat Indians in Pequot War.

1638 New Haven is founded by John Davenport and Thomas Eaton.

1639 Three River Towns of Hartford, Wethersfield, and Windsor unite the Colony of Connecticut; Fundamental Orders of Connecticut are adopted by the Colony of Connecticut.

1662 The Colony of Connecticut is officially chartered.

1665 New Haven becomes part of the Colony of Connecticut.

1701 Yale University is founded as Collegiate School.

1775 Revolutionary War begins.

1776 Nathan Hale is executed by British as a spy.

1781 Benedict Arnold leads British troops in raid on New London.

1784 Connecticut Emancipation Law is passed; children born to slaves would be free at age 25; America's first law school founded at New Litchfield.

1788 Connecticut becomes fifth state.

1794 Cotton gin is patented by Eli Whitney.

1818 New state constitution is ratified.

1839 First railroad goes into service in Connecticut; Charles Goodyear discovers vulcanization of rubber.

1841 U.S. Supreme Court decides in favor of the Africans who fought for their freedom en route to Cuba aboard the *Amistad*.

1848 Slavery ends in Connecticut.

1875 Hartford becomes state's only capital.

1882 Knights of Columbus is founded at New Haven.

1888 Centennial celebration is held.

1898 First car insurance in America is issued at Hartford.

1917 United States submarine base is established at Groton.

1954 First atomic submarine, the *Nautilus*, is launched at Groton.

1957 University of Hartford is founded.

1965 Present state constitution is adopted.

1966 Dinosaur tracks are found at Rocky Hill.

1974 Ella Grasso is elected governor.

1983 Major road-building program begins.

1984 Ellen Ash Peters becomes first woman named to Connecticut Supreme Court.

1990 Eunice S. Groark becomes the first woman lieutenant governor elected in Connecticut.

1991 State's first income tax is passed.

1992 Mashantucket Pequots open Foxwoods casino in Ledyard.

1996 Conneticut Supreme Court rules in favor of the plaintiffs in *Sheff v. O'Neill*; Mohegan tribe opens Mohegan Sun casino in Uncasville.

2000 Senator Joseph Lieberman becomes the first Jewish vice-presidential candidate in American history.

2001 Seventy-two Connecticut citizens die in terrorist bombings of the World Trade Center in New York City.

2004 M. Jodi Rell becomes the second woman governor in Connecticut after the resignation of Governor John Rowland.

ECONOMY

Agricultural Products: Apples, eggs, milk and dairy products, potatoes, poultry, strawberries, tobacco, greenhouse and nursery plants

Manufactured Products: Airplane engines, boats, brass products, clocks, electrical products, foods, helicopters, metal products, rubber products, silverware, submarines

Natural Resources: Clay, feldspar, gravel, sand, stone, traprock, garnet

Business and Trade: Communications, finance, insurance, real estate, transportation, wholesale and retail trade

Strawberries

Daffodil Festival New Britain holds this community festival in mid-April when about 500,000 daffodils are in bloom.

Silvermine Chamber Music Series From May through September, New Canaan hosts this series of live theater and music.

Branford Festival The popular vacation spot of Branford celebrates Father's Day each June with this three-day festival on the town green.

New Haven International Festival of Arts & Ideas Held on the New Haven Public Green in June, this festival presents diverse music, visual arts, and educational presentations for all ages.

Old Saybrook Arts and Crafts Show Artists from all over the state and 25,000 visitors arrive during the last weekend of July to set up booths in this historic town.

Taste of Old Saybrook The local restaurants set up booths along the town's sidewalks during July to give residents and visitors a chance to sample their favorite dishes. Taste everything from rich desserts to ethnic cuisines such as Thai.

Italian Festival The July celebration in Westport features Italian food, arts, and crafts.

New Haven Jazz Festival Every July and/or August, the town green swings to the sound of America's music, jazz.

Connecticut Agricultural Fair Contests, exhibits, rides, and music are among the attractions at this fair, held on the Goshen fairgrounds at the end of July.

Midsummer Festival On the first Saturday in August, visitors to the Lyme Academy of Fine Arts and other locations on Lyme Street can listen to live music, watch painting demonstrations, and buy students' artwork.

Chrysanthemum Festival During this month-long festival that begins in September, Bristol celebrates the arrival of autumn with a display of ethnic foods, cultures, and customs.

New London Literary, Art, Maritime and Food Festival Sponsored by Sail New London, this September event combines a love of the sea with great food and the arts.

Norwalk Oyster Festival Norwalk celebrates its important oyster industry with a three-day festival in September. Seafood is abundant, with plenty of oysters and clams to eat while enjoying the live entertainment. Kids' Cove features amusement rides, magic tricks, and lots of games.

Southington Apple Harvest Festival The last weekend in September and the first weekend in October are set aside for this celebration of the rich tastes and colors of autumn.

Connecticut Renaissance Faire Visitors can see magicians, puppeteers, and performances of Renaissance shows and try their skills in archery in Woodstock on weekends in September and October.

Festival of Traditional Folk, Dance and Music Held in Newtown in November, this festival celebrates traditions from the United States and around the world.

Main Street Stroll Old Saybrook hosts this winterfest each December. The highlight of the festival, the torchlight parade, gives participants the chance to walk back into colonial times along with fife and drum players.

STATE STARS

Dean Gooderham Acheson (1893–1971) was born in Middletown. As a statesman, he advised several American presidents, including Truman, Kennedy, and Johnson. He served as U.S. undersecretary of state from 1945 to 1947. As secretary of state from 1949 to 1952, he helped draft the Marshall Plan. In 1970 he received the Pulitzer Prize in history for *Present at the Creation*, his book about his service in the State Department.

Phineas Taylor (P. T.) Barnum (1810–1891) was America's greatest showman in the nineteenth century. He helped found the Ringling Brothers and Barnum & Bailey Circus, "The Greatest Show on Earth." He was born in Bethel.

P. T. Barnum

Paul Wayland Bartlett (1865–1925) was a sculptor born in New Haven. His most famous sculpture was *The Dying Lion*. He also executed a famous statue of Lafayette, the French hero of the Revolutionary War, which was given to France as a gift from the children of America.

Hiram Bingham (1875–1956) was a professor of archaeology at Yale when he discovered the Incan ruins at Machu Picchu in 1911. He served briefly as governor of Connecticut in 1925 and then served in the U.S. Senate from 1925 to 1933.

John Brown (1800–1859), a native of Torrington, was a dedicated abolitionist. In 1859 he led a group of slaves and supporters, including his two sons, in an unsuccessful raid on the federal armory at Harper's Ferry, Virginia. He was arrested, then put on trial and executed, but his antislavery speeches during his trial inspired others to oppose slavery.

Al Capp (1909–1979) was the creator of the famous comic strip "L'il Abner." He was born in New Haven as Alfred Gerald Caplin.

Glenn Close (1947–   ) is a successful screen and stage actress who was born in Greenwich. She starred in the hit films *The Big Chill* and *Fatal Attraction* and won a Tony Award for her role in *The Real Thing* in 1984.

John Brown

Roger Connor (1857–1931) starred for eighteen years in the National League as a first baseman, mostly for the New York Giants. At various times in his career, he led the league in batting, slugging, doubles, triples, home runs, and runs batted in. He was elected to the Baseball Hall of Fame in 1976. He was born in Waterbury.

Prudence Crandall (1803–1890) grew up in Canterbury, where she founded a successful girls' school in 1831. After Crandall accepted an African-American student, white citizens withdrew their children, so she operated her school solely for African Americans. Threats and violence forced her to close down, and she went to jail for breaking a new law passed in 1833 to make her school illegal. Throughout her life, she continued to teach and to oppose slavery and support women's rights. In 1886 the Connecticut state legislature sent Crandall a formal apology and awarded her an annual pension of $400.

Charles Goodyear (1800–1860) was an inventor born in New Haven. He discovered that heating, or vulcanizing, rubber would keep it from melting and sticking in hot weather. His invention made rubber practical for a number of new uses, especially for tires.

Dorothy Hamill

Dorothy Hamill (1956–   ) was born in Chicago, but her family moved to Riverside shortly after her birth. At age eight, the future Olympic figure-skating champion began training at a local ice rink. Known for her athletic speed and grace, Hamill developed a move called the "Hamill camel."

Katharine Hepburn (1907–2003), a native of Hartford, has been called the First Lady of Cinema and one of the finest actors of all time. During her sixty-year acting career, she showed her talent for both comedy and dramatic roles. Hepburn won a record-setting four Academy Awards after being nominated twelve times.

Katharine Hepburn

Charles Ives (1874–1954) was born in Danbury. After graduating from Yale, he ran an insurance business. In his spare time, Ives wrote music and eventually became a leading classical composer. Known for his unique and expressive style, he is called the Father of American music. Ives won the Pulitzer Prize in 1947 for his *Symphony No. 3.*

Steven Kellogg (1941–   ) was born in Norwalk. As a child he loved nature, writing, and art. This led him to a successful career illustrating and writing books for children. Kellogg wrote many of his more than ninety books at his farmhouse in Stoneybrook. Many of his works feature animals, including family pets.

John Mayer (1977–   ), a native of Bridgeport, became a Grammy-winning pop singer and songwriter. This singer-guitarist has recorded several top-selling CDs, including *Room for Squares* (2001), *Any Given Thursday* (2003), and *Heavier Things* (2003).

John Mayer

John Pierpont (J. P.) Morgan (1837–1913) was born in Hartford. He amassed one of America's greatest fortunes. As a financier, he helped organize some of the largest U.S. corporations, such as AT&T, General Electric, International Harvester, and U.S. Steel. He donated paintings, sculptures, and books to many libraries and museums.

Ralph Nader (1934–   ) was born in Winsted. After Nader earned a law degree from Harvard, he became interested in consumer protection. He wrote *Unsafe at Any Speed* (1965), which criticized the automobile industry and pushed for safer cars. The book was a best-seller and led to the passage of the National Traffic and Motor Vehicle Safety Act in 1966. Since then, Nader has influenced several key pieces of legislation. He launched a nonprofit agency, The Public Interest Research Group.

Frederick Law Olmsted (1822–1903) was a landscape architect born in Hartford. He designed New York City's Central Park and many other park spaces in urban areas across the country.

Eugene O'Neill (1888–1953) born in New York City, spent his boyhood summers in New London. Regarded by many as America's greatest playwright, he won the 1936 Nobel Prize in literature. His greatest play, *Long Day's Journey into Night*, is partly based on his own family and set in New London.

Rosa Ponselle (1897–1981) was an operatic soprano born in Meriden. She starred with the New York Metropolitan Opera from 1918 to 1937, appearing in *Don Giovanni*, *La Gioconda*, and *Aida*.

Meg Ryan (1961–   ) was born in Fairfield. She became one of the world's most popular actresses, best-known for her romantic comedies, including *Sleepless in Seattle* and *You've Got Mail*. Ryan has shown her versatility in dramatic films, including *Courage Under Fire* and *Against the Ropes*.

Meg Ryan

Eliss Ruley (1882–1959) was a self-taught African-American artist born in Norwich. He began painting in 1929 after an accident left him too disabled to continue in his former job. Ruley's work provide a unique view of small-town Connecticut, as well as scenes from native African-American life, as well as scenes from nature.

Roger Sherman (1721–1793), born in Newtown, Massachusetts, was the only colonial statesman to sign all four of the following documents: the Articles of Association, the Articles of Confederation, the Declaration of Independence, and the Constitution.

Benjamin Silliman (1799–1864) was one of the foremost American scientists of his day. A chemist and toxicologist who did groundbreaking work in the use of petroleum products, he helped found the National Academy of Sciences in 1863. He was born in North Stratford and taught for many years at Yale.

Venture Smith (1729?–1805) was one of East Haddam's best-known colonial residents. He was taken from his native Guinea in Africa at age eight. As a slave, he lived with several owners. From 1761 to 1765 he did extra fishing, farming, and wood chopping to buy his freedom. In 1798 he dictated his story to a local schoolteacher. Published as *A Narrative of the Life and Adventures of Venture, a Native of Africa*, it is a rare account of life for a first-generation African American in colonial days.

Benjamin Spock (1903–1998) is the pediatrician who wrote the best-selling nonfiction book of all time, *The Common Sense Book of Baby and Child Care*. Since it was first published in 1946, millions of American parents have consulted this book for advice on raising their children. Born in New Haven, Spock led opposition to U.S. involvement in the Vietnam War in the 1960s and was a third-party presidential candidate in 1972.

Harriet Beecher Stowe (1811–1896) was born in Litchfield. An abolitionist and author, her most famous book was *Uncle Tom's Cabin*, which was published in 1852. This enormously popular novel portrayed slavery as a morally evil system and helped influence the attitudes that led to the Civil War.

Noah Webster

Noah Webster (1758–1843) was born in Hartford. Educated at Yale, Webster became the foremost American expert on the English language. A lexicographer, lawyer, and newspaper publisher, Webster compiled the popular "blue-backed Spelling book" *Spelling Book* (1783) and the *American Dictionary of the English Language* (1828), which was the first American dictionary.

Elihu Yale (1649–1721) was an English philanthropist who donated books and other valuable items to the Collegiate School of Connecticut. The school was renamed Yale University in his honor in 1718.

TOUR THE STATE

Henry C. Bowen House (Woodstock) This Gothic revival house was built in 1846 and is known as Roseland Cottage or the Pink House. It contains one of the oldest bowling alleys in the United States.

Christopher Leffingwell House Museum (Norwich) Officers in the Continental Army, including George Washington, visited this patriot's home during the Revolutionary War. Historical furniture and artifacts from the period are on display in the house, which dates to 1675 and was purchased by Leffingwell in 1701.

Mohegan Indian Burial Ground (Norwich) This Native American resting place includes members of the family of Uncas.

Mohegan Park and Memorial Rose Garden (Norwich) Fishing, swimming, walking nature trails, and visiting the children's zoo are the most popular attractions in this nearly 380-acre park.

Mystic Aquarium & Institute in Exploration (Mystic) This aquarium is the state's largest, with permanent and changing exhibits that show thousands of living sea creatures, including seals, sea lions, and African black-footed penguins. Visitors can work with the staff during special contact programs with whales and penguins.

Mystic Seaport Museum (Mystic) This historical re-creation presents a glimpse of life in a nineteenth-century seaport. Its several exhibits, including period homes and shops, three ships, and a special Children's Museum, are spread over seventeen acres.

Mystic Seaport Museum

Fort Griswold State Park (Groton) The park is on the site of the fortress captured by the British during the Revolutionary War.

Submarine Force Library and Museum (Groton) Exhibits demonstrate how submarines developed and feature a model of Captain Nemo's *Nautilus* from Jules Verne's science-fiction novel *Twenty Thousand Leagues Under the Sea*. Operated by the U.S. Navy, the museum holds important documents and photographs.

Connecticut River Museum (Essex) At this museum you will find exhibits of steamboats, shipbuilding, and regional archaeology. A popular exhibit highlights the *Turtle*, which was built in 1776 and is said to be the first submarine.

Beardsley Zoo (Bridgeport) Visitors can take a peek at 120 species of animals in outdoor habitats, visit an indoor rain forest, or pet the animals in the New England farm setting of the Children's Zoo.

Discovery Museum (Bridgeport) Interactive art and science exhibits, including the *Challenger* Learning Center and a planetarium, encourage visitors to explore their environment.

Bruce Museum (Greenwich) This museum house more than 25,000 items in the categories of fine arts, cultural history, and environmental sciences. Permanent exhibits include Native American artifacts and costumes, while science galleries cover local history and geological finds.

Lockwood-Mathews Mansion Museum (Norwalk) Standing four stories high, this fifty-room stone mansion was built in 1864 for banker and investor LeGrand Lockwood. Visitors can see examples of Victorian wall stencils, inlaid woodwork, and marble floors, as well as fine furnishings and a collection of music boxes.

Monte Cristo Cottage (New London) The boyhood home of Eugene O'Neill was the setting for his famous play *Long Day's Journey into Night*.

Old Lighthouse Museum (Stonington) Old whaling and fishing equipment, along with antique toys and other historic items, are located in this stone lighthouse built in 1823.

Amistad Memorial (New Haven) This bronze sculpture outside city hall commemorates the Africans who fought for their freedom against the slave-traders who kidnapped them from their homeland.

Peabody Museum of Natural History (New Haven) Fossils of dinosaurs and prehistoric mammals are the attraction at this museum.

Eli Whitney Museum (Hamden) The numerous hands-on exhibits here include a water learning lab where visitors can operate valves and levers. A working model of the cotton gin is on display, and a covered bridge and a waterfall beautify the grounds.

New Canaan Nature Center (New Canaan) Forty acres of plants and animals in their natural habitats, as well as a solar greenhouse, await visitors to the center.

Danbury Railway Museum (Danbury) This museum includes a station restored to look as it would in 1903. The collection includes vintage railcars and boxcars, a locomotive, a sleeping car, and an observation car. Visitors can take short trips in the yard or ride into the Hudson River valley.

Mattatuck Museum (Waterbury) Charles Goodyear's rubber desk is one of the highlights of this museum, devoted to the industrial history of the area, social history, and works by Connecticut artists.

The Institute for American Indian Studies (Washington) Native American artifacts chronicle 12,000 years of Native American life in this area. A replica of a Native American village, a nature trail, and an archaeological site offer further glimpses into tribal life.

Mashantucket Museum and Research Center (Mashantucket) This center is the most comprehensive facility of its kind in the world. Permanent and changing exhibits show Native American history in the United States and Canada over the past 18,000 years. Visitors can also attend live performances that showcase Native American music and dance.

New England Air Museum (Windsor Locks) Vintage and modern aircraft, as well as many different exhibits, will thrill aviation buffs of all ages.

Connecticut Fire Museum (East Windsor) The museum houses a collection of antique fire equipment, including a fire sleigh, fire trucks, and memorabilia.

Connecticut Trolley Museum (East Windsor) Visitors can actually ride 3 miles on an antique trolley, as well as view trolleys and railroad cars dating from 1869 to 1947.

Lutz Children's Museum (Manchester) Hands-on exhibits about art, history, science, and nature make this museum unique. The fifty-three-acre nature center features a variety of wildlife habitats, where visitors can see small native, domestic, and exotic animals.

Lime Rock Park (Salisbury) This park features the famous Lime race-track, with special events on Memorial Day and the Fourth of July and a fall festival. Annual races include the world-class sports-car and stock-car races.

Dinosaur State Park (Rocky Hill) More than five hundred dinosaur footprints are on view at this geodome exhibit center, where visitors can make their own cast of an actual dinosaur footprint.

Harriet Beecher Stowe House and Library (Hartford) The actual home of the famous abolitionist and author of *Uncle Tom's Cabin* provides a unique perspective on American history.

Mark Twain House (Hartford) Mark Twain made this Victorian Gothic mansion his home for seventeen years. It was here that he wrote *Huckleberry Finn* and *A Connecticut Yankee in King Arthur's Court.*

Find Out More

If you would like to find out more about Connecticut, look in your school library, local public library, bookstore, or video store for the following titles.

BOOKS

Campbell, Susan and Bill Heald. *Connecticut Curiosities: Quirky Characters, Roadside Oddities & Other Offbeat Stuff*. Guilford, CT: Globe Pequot, 2002.

Hardy, David, et al. *50 Hikes in Connecticut: Hikes and Walks from the Berkshires to the Coast*. Woodstock, VT: Backcountry Guides, 2002.

Marsh, Carole. *The Connecticut Experience*. Bath, NC: Gallopade Publishing Group, 2000.

———. *Connecticut Native Americans: A Kid's Look at Our State's Chiefs, Tribes, Reservations, Powwows, Lore and More from the Past and Present*. Bath, NC: Gallopade Publishing Group, 2004.

Pell, Ed. *Connecticut: Land of Liberty*. Mankato, MN: Capstone Press, 2003.

Ritchie, David and Deborah. *Connecticut: Off the Beaten Path, A Guide to Unique Places*. Guilford, CT: Globe Pequot, 2002.

Wiener, Roberta, and James R. Arnold. *Connecticut: The History of Connecticut Colony*. Chicago: Raintree, 2004.

VIDEOS

Benedict Arnold, A Question of Honor. New York: A & E Home Video, 2003.

The Connecticut River. Wheeling, IL: Film Ideas, Inc., 2001.

Connecticut Seasons of Light. New York: Betsy White Enterprises, 2003.

The Town of Greenwich. Greenwich, CT. Director/Producer James Thomas, 2001.

Mark Twain's Neighborhood: Nook Farm. CPTV. Monterey Media, Inc., 2001.

WEB SITES

The Connecticut Historical Society
www.chs.org/
Gather information on Connecticut's history, genealogy, and online exhibits.

Connecticut
www.connecticut.com/
Find out about tourism, state government, and the history of Connecticut and view photos from this site's photo gallery.

Connecticut Committee on Culture & Tourism
www.tourism.state.ct.us
Information on this site is about getaways and special events throughout the state.

ConneCTkids
www.kids.state.ct.us/index.htm
This site is dedicated to exploring all that is Connecticut, including links to Connecticut schools and libraries, puzzles, and news.

Index

Page numbers in **boldface** are illustrations and charts.

Acheson, Dean Gooderham, 126
African Americans, 41–43, 51, 80
agriculture, 35, 50, 85, **93,** 94–95, 123
aircraft industry, 90, 91–92
American Clock and Watch Museum, 50
American Heritage River Initiative, 23
Amistad (Spanish slave ship), 43
Amistad Memorial, 136
Andros, Edmund, 34
attractions, 101–113, 133–138
Audubon Center, 103

Barkhamsted Reservoir, 10
Barnum Museum, 102
Barnum, Phineas Taylor (P.T.), 126, **126**
Bartlett, Paul Wayland, 127
Battle of Stonington (song), 44–45
Beardsley Zoological Gardens, 102, 135
Bingham, Hiram, 127
Bishop, Sarah, 16
Bolton, Conn., 112
Branford, Conn., 104
Bridgeport, Conn., 62–63
Brown, John, 127, 127
Bruce Museum, 135
Bulfinch, Charles, 108
Bush-Holley House, 39
Bushnell, David, 41
business, finance and trade industries, **84,** 86, 89, 94, 123
Buttolph-Williams House, 39

Canterbury, Conn., 112
Capp, Al, 127
casinos, 66, 68

caves/caving, 16
central Connecticut, 108–111
Charles E. Wheeler Wildlife Management Area, 14
Charles II of England, 34
Charles W. Morgan (whaling vessel), 51
Charter Oak, 34
Christopher Leffingwell House Museum, 134
Cinque, Joseph, 43
civil rights movement, 81
Civil War, 51
climate, 17–18, 117
Close, Glenn, 127
Colony of Connecticut, 32, 34
Colt, Samuel, 47
Comprehensive Conservation and Management Plan, 26
Connecticut Fire Museum, 137
Connecticut Historical Society Museum, 108
Connecticut River, 10, **11,** 22–24, **23**
Connecticut River Museum, 41, 135
Connecticut Trolley Museum, 138
Connecticut Valley, The (Thomas Chambers), **28**
Connor, Roger, 128
conservation, 22–24, 26–27
Cornwall, Conn., 111, **111**
Corsair fighter plane, **92**
Coventry, Conn., 112
Crandall, Prudence, 112, 128
crime rates, 60, 62–63
crops, 35, 50, 94–95, 123
cultural influences, 69–70

dams and dikes, 22
Danbury Railway Museum, 137
Dinosaur State Park, 138

Discovery Museum, 102, 135
Dodd, Christopher, 81

economy
1800s, 47
1900s, 52-53
agriculture industry, 94–95, 123
aircraft industry, 90, 91–92
business, finance and trade industries, **84,** 86, 89, 94, 123
casinos, 66, 68
fishing and aquaculture, 95–96
gross state product (2003), **87**
jobs/employment, 97–99
manufacturing industry, 50, 87–89, 123
military, 90–92
natural resources, 10–12, 123
shipbuilding, 90
tourist industry, 85
education, 35–36, 38, 68, 81–83
Eli Whitney Museum, 136
Elizabeth Park Rose Gardens, 110
Ellsworth, Oliver, 46
Elmwood House, 39
employment, 60, 62–63, 97–99
environmental concerns, 22–24, 26–27, 96
European settlers/colonists, 30–32, 35–36, 38–39

Fairfield County, 102–103
farming, 35, 50, 85, 94–95, 123
Faude, Wilson (Bill), 108
festivals, fairs and celebrations, **67,** 69, 70, 124–126
Fish Family Farm Creamery and Dairy, 112
forests, **14,** 14–15
Fort Griswold Battlefield State Park, 106, 135

Foxwoods casino, 66
Freeman, Jordan, 41
Fuller Brush Company, 89
Fuller, Alfred C., 89
Fundamental Agreement, 32
Fundamental Orders, 32

geography
    borders/boundaries, 9
    facts, 117
    lakes, rivers & streams, 9–10
    rocks, 10–12, **12**
    woods/forests, **14,** 14–15
Geology Park, 112
Gillette's Castle, 104
Gillette, William, 104
Gold Coast, 60, **60,** 102–103
Goodspeed Opera House, 104
Goodyear, Charles, 50, 128
government
    Clean Water/Clean Air Act, 26
    Connecticut Compromise, 46
    executive branch, 74–75
    Fundamental Orders, 32
    judicial branch, 77–78
    legislative branch, 75
    local, 78, 80
    Puritans of New Haven, 32
    state capitol building, **72,** 108,
        109, 110
    state symbols, 114–115
    statehouse (old), 108
    taxes, 75
    voting, 80–81
Grasso, Ella Tambussi, 74, 76, **76**
Groton, Conn., 106

Hadlyme, Conn., 104
Hale, Nathan, 112
Hamill, Dorothy, 128, **128**
Harkness Tower, **37**
Harriet Beecher Stowe House and
    Library, 138
Hartford, Conn., 32, **33,** 63,
    108–111
Haynes, Lemuel, 41
Henry C. Bowen House, 133
Hepburn, Katharine, 129, **129**
Hooker, Thomas, 32, **33**
horses/horse shows, 70

Housatonic River, 10

immigrants, 51–52
Institute for American Indian
    Studies, 137
Ives, Charles, 129

James II of England, 34
jobs, 97–99
Johnson, William Samuel, 46
Judson, Andrew, 43

Kellogg, Steven, 129
Kimberlin Nature Education, 103
King Philip's War, 35

lakes, rivers & streams, 9–10
landscape, 111
Leatherman Cave, 16
Leatherman, The, 16
Lieberman, Joseph, 81
lifestyles, 60, 62, 111
Lime Rock Park, 138
Little Red Schoolhouse, 36
Lockwood-Mathews Mansion
    Museum, 136
Long Island Sound, **17,** 24, **25,**
    26–27
Lutz Children's Museum, 138
Lyme disease, 21

manufacturing industry, 50,
    52–53, 87–89, **93,** 123
maps
    attractions, **107**
    county, **79**
    land and water, **13**
    population density, **61**
    resources, **93**
    road, **2**
Maritime Aquarium, 102, **103**
Mark Twain House, 138
Mashantucket Museum and
    Research Center, 137
Mattatuck Museum, 137
Mayer, John, 130, **130**
Middlesex County, 104–105
military, 90–92
Milner, Thurman, 80

mining, 10–12
Mohegan Indian Burial Ground,
    134
Mohegan Park and Memorial Rose
    Garden, 134
Mohegan Sun casino, 68, **68**
Monte Cristo Cottage, 136
museums, 41, 102, 106, 108, 111,
    112, 134–138
Mystic Aquarium & Institute in
    Exploration, 134
Mystic Seaport Museum, 134

Nader, Ralph, 130
Nathan Hale Homestead, 112
Native Americans
    and settlers/colonists, 30–31
    early tribes, 29–30
    festivals, **67**
    King Philip's War, 35
    Mohegans, 66, 68, 71, 134
    Pequot War, 30–31, **31**
    population, 29, 66
    reservations, 66
natural resources, 10–12, **93,** 123
nature centers, 103
Naval Submarine Base, **91**
New Canaan Nature Center, 136
New England Air Museum, 137
New England Carousel Museum,
    111
New Haven, Conn., 32, 103–104
nicknames (state), 32, 39, 48, 74

O'Neill, Eugene, 131, 136
Old Lighthouse Museum, 136
Olmsted, Frederick Law, 131

parks, 14
Peabody Museum of Natural
    History, 104, 136
peddlers, **48,** 48–49
Pepperidge Farm Company, 89
Pequot War, 30–31, **31**
Pierpont, John, 36
Pierpont, John Morgan (J.P.), 130
plant life, 14–15, 19, 117–118, 120
pollution, 22–24, 24, 26–27, 96
Ponselle, Rosa, 131

population
    African American, 41, 57
    Asian, 57–58
    density, 58, **61**
    diversity, 56–59
    growth (1720-2000), **46**
    Hungarian, 58
    immigrant, 52, 56–59
    Native American, 29, 57
    state, 22, 110
    ten largest cities, **110**
poverty, 60, 62, 81
Project Oceanology, 106
Prudence Crandall Museum, 112
Puritans, 32
Purple Heart Museum, 41

railway system, 47, 101
Rell, Jodi, 74–75, **75**
Revolutionary War, 39–41
Ribicoff, Abraham, 22
roadways, 47, 101
Rowland, John, 74–75
Rudkin, Margaret, 89
Ruley, Eliss, 131–132
Ryan, Meg, 131

schools, 35–36, 38, 68, 81–83
segregation, 83
September 11, 2001, 53
settlers/colonists, 30–32, 35–36, 38–39
Sheff, Milo, 83
Sheffield Island Lighthouse, **100**

Sherman, Roger, 46, 132
shipbuilding industry, 50, 90
shipping industry, 10
Sikorsky, Igor, 92
silk workers, **88**
Silliman, Benjamin, 132
Simsbury, Conn., 111–112
slavery, 41–43
Smith, Venture, 132
Special Olympic Games, 71
spelunking, 16
Spock, Benjamin, 132
sports, 70–71
state symbols, 114–115
steamboats, 47, **47**
stone walls, 12, **12**
Storrs, Conn., 112
Stowe, Harriet Beecher, 133
Submarine Force Library and Museum, 135
succotash (recipe), 65

taxes, 75
terrorism, 53
Terry, Eli, 50
Thames River, 10
timeline, historic, 120–123
Tolland County, 112
tourist industry, 85
trade/trading posts, 10, 30, 48–49, 85
transportation systems, 22, 47, 90–92, 101
Treat, Robert, 34

Trumbull, John, 74, 104
Trumbull, Jonathan, 40, 74, **74**
Turtle (submarine), 40–41

U.S. Navy Submarine Force Museum, 41
unemployment, 60, 62–63, 97–99
Union Bank of Switzerland, **84**
University of Connecticut, 112
USS *Nautilus,* 106, **106**

village greens, 111

Wadsworth Atheneum, 108
Washington, George, 39, 41
weather, 17–18, 117
Webster, Noah, 133, **133**
Weicker, Lowell, 75
whaling industry, 50–51, 106
Whitfield House, 39
Whitney, Eli, 50, 136
wildlife, 14, **19**, 19–21, **20**, 22, 24, **26**, 26–27, 118, **119**
Winthrop, John, Jr., 34, 74
World War I, 52
World War II, 52

Yale Center for British Art and British Studies, 104
Yale University, 36, **37**, 38
Yale University Art Gallery, 104
Yale, Elihu, 38, 133
Yale, Linus, 50
Yankee Doodle (song), 116

ABOUT THE AUTHOR

Victoria Sherrow has written many stories and articles, as well as picture books and numerous works of nonfiction for young readers. She has written biographies, covered historical subjects, science, and social issues. She lives in Westport, Connecticut.